MASTERGUIDE

BASIC MASTERCLASS

TIPS & TRICKS ON
PHOTOSHOP
ELEMENTS
2024

"A Practical Manual To Master Photo Editing In Photoshop Elements"

TODD LEMMINGS

LEGAL NOTICE

TABLE OF CONTENTS

INTRODUCTION

Photoshop Elements is one of the prominent software used for photo editing and is massively used in the photography and design industries after Adobe Photoshop. It is a graphic editing program that was created to create and modify digital content such as pictures, videos, and photos. The most recent version of Photoshop Elements was launched on Oct 19, 2023; Photoshop Elements 2024.

To introduce you to the fundamentals of Photoshop Elements 2024, This manual will take you step-by-step through learning how to use Photoshop Elements and all of its fascinating features as a beginner and an intermediate user.

To get the most out of this user manual, make sure your computer is in good working order and that you have a dependable internet connection.

As you go through this user manual, I wish you luck and satisfaction.

CHAPTER ONE
INTRODUCTION TO PHOTOSHOP ELEMENTS 2024

Overview Of Photoshop Elements 2024

Adobe Photoshop Elements 2024 is the most recent version of Adobe's popular photo-editing software for home users. It is designed to be affordable and easy to use, with various capabilities that can help users edit, enhance, and share their photographs. The official release took place on October 19, 2023.

Adobe Photoshop Element is a one-time purchase that does not require a recurring subscription. Content-aware cropping, AI-powered one-click subject selection, automated image colorization, and skin smoothing are just a few of the numerous features available in Adobe Photoshop Element. Both Mac and Windows machines can use it.

To offer a more effective user experience, additional features have been added to improve it. It provides a straightforward approach to getting started with instructions on quickly making outstanding picture creations, effects, designs, prints, etc. Some of the new features are listed below.

- **Improved UI layout**: Photoshop Elements 2024's user interface has been improved to satisfy consumers' aesthetic demands.

- **Web and Mobile Companion Apps:** The version has a mobile and web app. Moreover, import images from a larger variety of files and folders on your phone. With this, you can sync across the Elements Organizer and the web and mobile companion apps.

- **Creating Photo Reels**: Photo reels, with their text, effects, and graphics, allow you to scroll through your finest images swiftly. To make sharing easier, save them as MP4s or GIFs. This tool allows you to present your greatest photos exceptionally.

- **Support for New File Formats**: Photoshop Elements 2024 supports two new file formats: HEIC and HEIF.
- **Quick Actions**: You may immediately change the tone, remove backgrounds, adjust the white balance, and more with just one click on Quick Actions.

- **Auto Selections with One Click**: Improving or replacing a chosen location is simple when you use the automatic option.

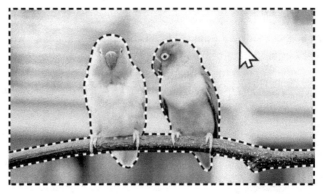

- **Stylized Texts**: With this new function, you can now create appealing texts for your projects and ideas

- **AI-powered Color Match**: With this feature, the color and tone of one photo are automatically matched to another. This can be useful for making collages or matching a photo's color to a particular theme.

- **New Filters**: Black & White, Color Match, and Artistic Filter are available in the software's filter menu. An artistic filter produces a sketchbook or painting-like look. A grayscale image can be produced using a black-and-white filter, which offers several ways to adjust the grayscale image's contrast and intensity. Meanwhile, Color Match can be used to add color to a photograph.
- **Free Access to Adobe Stock**: With Photoshop Elements, you can experiment with different backgrounds, create collages, or design motivational quote graphics using thousands of gorgeous stock photos. This feature lets you quickly and easily access thousands of free Adobe Stock images. You can change your background image using the free Adobe Stock image. The Quote Graphics also provides access to Adobe Stock. Navigate to the *File menu*, select *Adobe Stock Search*, and look through the library for the desired picture.

- **Enhanced Organizer and Improved Performance:** With several enhancements to the program's speed and responsiveness, Photoshop Elements 2024 has been performance-optimized.

The minimum requirements for Photoshop Elements 2024 are displayed in the box below.

Windows	macOS
Processor with AMD equivalent or Intel 6th Generation or later and support for SSE4.1.	Intel CPUs from the sixth generation or later.
Windows 7 and 8.1 are not supported; only 64-bit versions of Microsoft Windows 10 (version 22H2) or Windows 11 (version 22H2) are.	Apple CPUs using macOS 12, macOS 13, and silicon M1 generation or later (13.4 or later)
8 GB of RAM and 8 GB of free hard drive space are required for installing apps; additional space is required for temporary files and downloading internet material while using and installing products (installs cannot be made on removable flash drives or volumes with case-sensitive file systems).	The application requires 8 GB of RAM and 6 GB of free hard drive space to install; additional space is required for temporary files and internet content downloads during the installation and operation of the product (it cannot be installed on removable flash drives or volumes that use case-sensitive file systems).
Resolution of the display: 1280 x 800 (at 100% scale factor)	Resolution of the display: 1280 x 800 (at 100% scale factor)
Display driver compatible with Microsoft DirectX 12.	You must have an internet connection to activate the product and download features and online content.
Internet connection necessary for product activation and feature and content downloads	

How Tips and Tricks in Photo Editing Will Up Your Editing Skills

Image enhancement and manipulation is referred to as picture editing. With the use of editing, you can produce the greatest possible image that is as near to your original vision as feasible or better perhaps.

Improving the quality of an image is one of the main advantages of using Photoshop Elements for photo editing. Whether you are a beginner or a professional, you want the finest possible quality in your photos. You can modify a picture's brightness, contrast, and saturation with Photoshop Elements to give it a more lively and appealing appearance. You can also refine the image by removing extraneous elements or imperfections.

Credibility building in a challenging environment is one of the main advantages of photo editing, particularly for startups. Especially for e-commerce businesses, photo editing is crucial. The product's image has a direct impact on sales figures and consumer perception. Research has shown that superior imagery performs better than stock photos and lower-quality imagery and that using more high-quality images leads to higher conversion rates and the development of consumer trust.

Your work will also seem more professional if you use Photoshop Elements for picture editing.

Photoshop Elements offers the added benefit of time and cost savings for photo processing. You may take several photographs and select the best one to edit, saving hours of trying to get the ideal shot.

In this book, you will be learning the following...

- **Easy Navigation of Photo Elements Interface**: There are principles to using every feature in the Photoshop Elements design software from the Home screen to each workspace that must be mastered to save time and effort while carrying out an operation. Most of these operations are discussed and addressed in this book including shortcut keys of tools and some other operations to allow seamless operations.

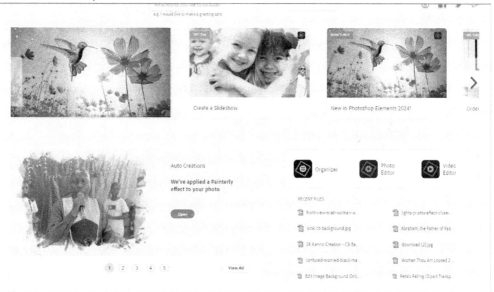

- **Creation Of Photo Projects**: Available in Photoshop Elements are features to create photo projects like Slideshows, Photo Reels, Greeting Cards, etc, and how to create all these seamlessly is thoroughly discussed in this book.

- **Resizing Images and Extending Photo Backgrounds**: Resizing an image means changing its size. By extending your photo background, you can add text and graphics and alter the image's orientation.

RESIZE YOUR PHOTO
Easily resize your photo for printing or posting to the web.

EXTEND BACKGROUND
Extend the background of your photo.

- **Straightening** and **Cropping**: While straightening an image means adjusting its horizon, cropping an image means removing some of its normally peripheral parts to emphasize the subject or improve the composition in various ways.

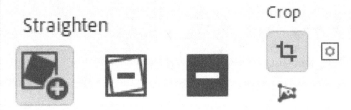

- **Fixing and Enhancing Photographs**: Photoshop Elements has commands and choices for improving and repairing a photograph's longevity and quality, with a few upgrades made to them in the 2024 version of Photoshop Elements.

PERFECT LANDSCAPE

Replace the sky, remove haze, erase unwanted objects, and more.

LIGHTEN AND DARKEN

Independently adjust the shadows, highlights, and mid-tones of your photo to get the perfect exposure.

BRIGHTNESS AND CONTRAST

Easily correct the brightness and contrast of your photo.

CORRECT SKIN TONE

Remove a color cast from your photo to get perfect skin tones.

- **Recomposing Photographs**: This allows you to quickly resize your photo without losing significant features.

RECOMPOSE

Easily resize your photo without losing the most important parts.

- **Removing people and unwanted elements from a photograph:** With the Object Removal command, you may precisely remove undesired components from a photo without causing the entire image to become distorted.

OBJECT REMOVAL

Make unwanted objects vanish.

- **Fixing Hue/Color Problems**: To improve the color expression of a photograph or image and fix color issues, Photoshop Elements offers enhancing features. You can resolve any problems with contrast, color, and clarity with these features.

ENHANCE COLOR
Fine-tune and enhance the colors in your photo.

LOMO CAMERA EFFECT
Easily give your photo that high-contrast, heavily saturated Lomo camera look.

REMOVE A COLOR CAST
Remove unwanted color tinting to reveal your photos' true colors.

- **Working with Auto Fixes**: With the help of these features in Photoshop Elements, you can save time and effort making adjustments, enhancing, and fixing photographs.

Auto Smart Fix	Alt+Ctrl+M
Auto Smart Tone...	Alt+Ctrl+T
Auto Levels	Shift+Ctrl+L
Auto Contrast	Alt+Shift+Ctrl+L
Auto Haze Removal	Alt+Ctrl+A
Auto Color Correction	Shift+Ctrl+B
Auto Shake Reduction	
Auto Sharpen	
Auto Red Eye Fix	Ctrl+R

- **Turning Photographs into live videos**: In addition to improving your photos, you can also apply live effects to any area of the picture or the entire one (i.e., turning it into a motion or animation).

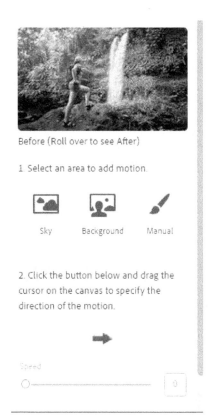

Before (Roll over to see After)

1. Select an area to add motion.

Sky   Background   Manual

2. Click the button below and drag the cursor on the canvas to specify the direction of the motion.

Speed

- **Making A Photo Collage**: Combining many photos can produce a single image. Sophisticated auto-crop is used to construct photo collages, with the focus being on the face, which is the most obvious component of the image, and placing it within the collage frames.

CHAPTER TWO
WORKSPACE AND ENVIRONMENT

The Home Screen

The Home Screen is the first user interface that shows up on your screen when you run Photoshop Elements.

The user's home screen displays automatically generated photos, videos, and slide shows created by the software using the imported media. You may switch workspaces, view recently opened files, find inspiration for new projects, browse humorous editing projects, and ask the Adobe community a question from the home screen.

Contained in the Home Screen are the below.

- **Carousel of Cards**: Information on new features, tasks, and inspirational ideas is accessible to users through a carousel of cards located in the upper section of the Home Screen. Clicking the arrows on the left and right edges of the carousel allows you to go around it.

The three card categories in the carousel are **Explore**, **Try This**, and **What's New**.

Explore:

This tag allows you to investigate particular aspects of the Photoshop Element application. To utilize this function, click the View button.

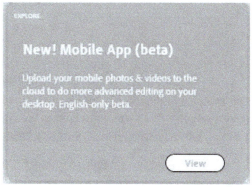

Try This:

You can access a variety of fascinating features by clicking on this green tag. The way you interact with Photoshop Elements and the features you use determine how these features are shown and updated. Click the Try button to test any of these features.

What's New:

Information on recent additions to the Photoshop Element program is available through this blue tag. You must click the Open Link symbol to use these resources.

- **Search Bar**: This interface button allows you to rapidly search for tutorials and help files for various functionalities. It is situated at the top of the Home Screen. The search bar can be used by typing the appropriate keyword into it and hitting the Enter key on your keyboard. The relevant results will then show up on the Home Screen as thumbnails and hyperlinks.

> What would you like to do today?
>
> e.g. I would like to make a greeting card

- **Auto Creation**: These are found at the bottom of the Home Screen and are generated automatically by the software utilizing the media that has been imported into the Elements. Selecting Add Media from the Auto Creation menu will allow you to add media to Auto Creations. By selecting View All or the number icon beneath the Auto Creations thumbnail, you may see every auto-created project, including picture collages, slideshows, and video collages.

- **Recent Files**: The recently worked-on project files are visible on the Home Screen. You can immediately resume working on the project using this symbol. The Photo Editor's open images are shown in this window.

- **Organizer**: On the right side of the Home Screen is where you'll find the Organizer. Use this to import, explore, and organize images to maintain a functional and well-organized image library. You can find, sort, rank, and categorize your photos with the features in the Organizer.

- **Photo Editor**: The tools for taking and processing pictures are in this area. These include tools for image correction, brightness, color, and other things.
  The tools for taking and processing pictures are in this area. These include tools for image correction, brightness, color, and other things.

- **Video Editor**: This makes Photoshop Element's editing tools and videos available to you.

- **Social Media Icons**: Located on the upper left side of the Home Screen, it contains the official social media accounts and websites for Photoshop Elements.

The Photo Editor

The Photo Editor is one of the most crucial tools in the Photoshop section. The center of photo editing is the photo editor.

You may adjust the contrast and brightness, crop, resize, rotate, and apply filters to your photographs using its various capabilities. You may also add text and shapes to your photographs with the Photo Editor. As was already noted, the Photo Editor has tools for adding effects, modifying brightness and color, fixing images, and more.

By selecting the Photo Editor icon from the Home Screen, you may open the Photo Editor and see the interface on your screen.

The Photo Editor is made up of three editing workspaces. Namely, **Quick, Guided**, and **Advanced**. To access this mode, click on them.

Quick   Guided   Advanced

Quick Mode is the most minimal and basic workspace in the Photo Editor. It offers fewer editing options and tools in comparison to the other workspaces.

Guided Mode is the second workspace in the Photo Editor. It's better than Quick Mode, but not as equipped as the Advanced Mode. This workspace allows for the creation of a wide range of preset effects that function as a wizard-like interface. In the Guided Edit mode, you may select the basic editing settings for your photographs and let the computer take care of the rest.

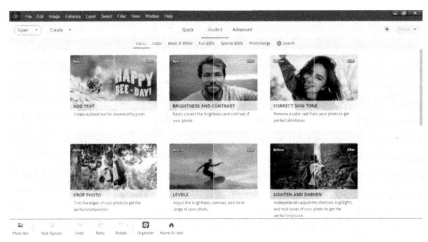

The six categories that comprise the guided edits in guided mode are **Basic, Color, Black & White, Fun Edits, Special Edits, and Photomerge**.

Basics   Color   Black & White   Fun Edits   Special Edits   Photomerge   Search

- **Basic**: You may add text to a photo and manipulate the images using features like brightness and contrast, levels, cropping, and skin tone correction with this edit.

ADD TEXT

Create stylized text for shareworthy posts

BRIGHTNESS AND CONTRAST

Easily correct the brightness and contrast of your photo.

CORRECT SKIN TONE

Remove a color cast from your photo to get perfect skin tones.

CROP PHOTO

Trim the edges of your photo to get the perfect composition

LEVELS

Adjust the brightness, contrast, and tonal range of your photo.

LIGHTEN AND DARKEN

Independently adjust the shadows, highlights, and mid-tones of your photo to get the perfect exposure

MOVE & SCALE OBJECT

Easily select an object and change its position, size, and more.

OBJECT REMOVAL

Make unwanted objects vanish.

RESIZE YOUR PHOTO

Easily resize your photo for printing or posting to the web.

ROTATE AND STRAIGHTEN

Easily level out the horizon of your photo.

SHARPEN

Make your photo crisp and crystal clear.

VIGNETTE EFFECT

Darken the corners of your photo to highlight the subject

- **Color**: You may use this to change the color of your images with features like enhanced color, Lomo camera effect, cast color removal, saturated film effect, etc.

ENHANCE COLOR

Fine-tune and enhance the colors in your photo.

LOMO CAMERA EFFECT

Easily give your photo that high-contrast, heavily saturated Lomo camera look.

REMOVE A COLOR CAST

Remove unwanted color tinting to reveal your photos' true colors.

SATURATED FILM EFFECT

Add a classic saturated slide-film feel to your photo.

- **Black & White**: Using features like B&W color pop and B&W selection, you can utilize this edition to turn a section of the complete shot black and white.

- **Fun Edits**: The Fun edit allows you to apply interesting effects to your images, such as double exposure, multi-photo text, making memes, and more.

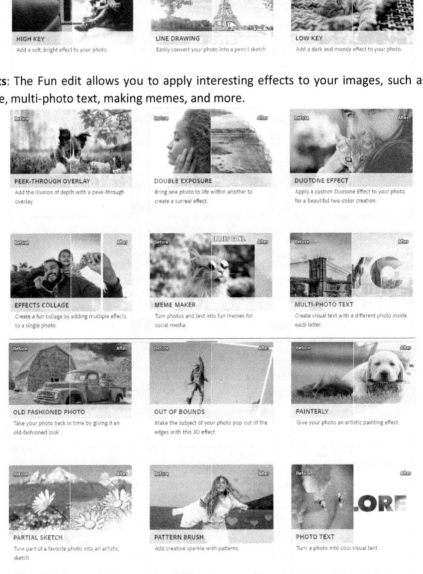

PICTURE STACK

Give your photo the feeling of a creative collage.

POP ART

Transform your photo into a fun and colorful Pop Art masterpiece.

PUZZLE EFFECT

Convert your photo into a jigsaw puzzle.

REFLECTION

Add a reflection to create an interesting look.

SHAPE OVERLAY EFFECT

Add a shape overlay effect to create an artistic look.

SPEED EFFECT

Add some action with motion blur

SPEED PAN

Add a motion blur to the background to create the impression of speed.

ZOOM BURST EFFECT

Add some motion and action to your photo with this classic effect.

- **Special Edits**: You can apply creative and artistic effects to your photos with the Special edit feature by utilizing tools such as the Orton effect, ideal landscape, depth of field, frame creator, and others.

DEPTH OF FIELD

Make your subject stand out by blurring the background.

EXTEND BACKGROUND

Extend the background of your photo.

FRAME CREATOR

Create a new frame file from your own design

ORTON EFFECT

Add a soft, dreamy look to your photo.

PERFECT LANDSCAPE

Replace the sky, remove haze, erase unwanted objects, and more.

PERFECT PET

Create perfect pet pics.

PERFECT PORTRAIT
Make your portrait photos flawless and stunning.

RECOMPOSE
Easily resize your photo without losing the most important parts.

REPLACE BACKGROUND
Change the background of your photo.

RESTORE OLD PHOTO
Transform an old scanned photo to give it a fresh and flawless look.

SCRATCHES AND BLEMISHES
Fix small flaws in your photo.

TEXT AND BORDER OVERLAY
Embellish special photos with polished borders and text.

TILT-SHIFT
Add a "miniature effect" without the need for a tilt-shift lens.

WATERCOLOR EFFECT
Create a Watercolor Effect for your photo.

- **Photomerge**: Connecting or combining different photos with the Photomerge Edit tool allows you to generate a new image. Photomerge editing includes features including Photomerge composition, Photomerge exposure, Photomerge faces, and Photomerge group.

PHOTOMERGE COMPOSE
Extract an object from one photo and add it to another.

PHOTOMERGE EXPOSURE
Blend shots with different exposures to get perfect lighting every time.

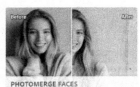

PHOTOMERGE FACES
Have fun by blending faces from two different photos into one.

PHOTOMERGE GROUP SHOT
Make sure everyone in your group shot is smiling and has their eyes open by blending multiple shots into one.

PHOTOMERGE SCENE CLEANER
Easily remove moving objects, like cars, from a series of photos.

PHOTOMERGE PANORAMA
Create a panoramic photo by stitching together multiple photos.

The **Search Bar** yet negligible but should not be neglected. The Guided Edit Search window in Photoshop Elements can be used to find the relevant Guided Edit. Search to discover new activities or to locate what you want to do fast. The Guided Edit Search window in Photoshop Elements can be used to find the relevant Guided Edit. Search to discover new activities or to locate what you want to do fast and simple.

Advanced Mode is the most sophisticated workspace in the Photo Editor, but it is also the most intuitive. It provides a wider range of tools—and menu options—than the workspace modes that were previously covered. As the name implies, it is advanced indeed.

Navigating The Photo Editor

The **Image Window** serves as the primary workspace for the Photoshop Element program. The numerous images that are opened and made are displayed on the image window's canvas.

The features to explore in the image window are listed below.

- **File Name**: The status bar above the image window shows the filename of each file that is opened in the image window.

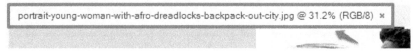

- **Magnificent Box**: You may immediately view how an image is zoomed in or out with this option. It is situated exactly above the Taskbar.

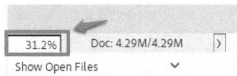

- **Information Box**: The information box sits next to the magnificent box and lets you select the data to show by selecting options that open in a pop-up menu.

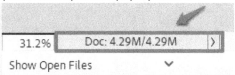

The following are the options that can be found in the information box:

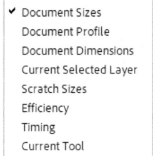

- ⬍ **Document Size**: This option displays details about the size and resolution of the files that are stored.
- ⬍ **Document Profile**: This option shows the file's color profile.
- ⬍ **Document Dimension**: This displays the real size of the document in the desired measurement unit, such as inches.
- ⬍ **Current Selected Layer**: You can select Current Selected Layer as a readout by clicking and selecting a layer in the Layer panel.
- ⬍ **Scratch Sizes**: The memory utilized by each open document is shown by this option.
- ⬍ **Efficiency**: This controls the number of operations performed as opposed to using the scratch disk. The RAM is exhausted when the value approaches 100%. When the percentage drops below 100%, the scratch disk is used.
- ⬍ **Timing**: This displays the amount of time needed to complete the last task.
- ⬍ **Current Tools**: This window displays the tool's name chosen from the Touch panel.

- **Scroll bar**: You see the Scroll bar when you enlarge an image. Use the scroll bar, the scroll arrows, or the Hand tool from the Toolbar to move the image within the window image.

The **Photo Bin** is situated at the foot of the workspace, immediately beneath the Image Window before the Tool Options Panel.

A glimpse of the photos that are open in the Photo Editor at the moment is shown in the Photo Bin. This tab has two options: **Show Selected Files in Organizer** and **Show Open Files**.

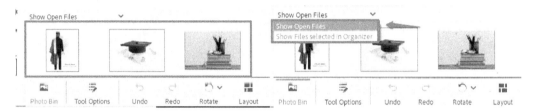

The Photo Bin displays a thumbnail of every image that has been seen in the Image window. You can reorganize a large number of open photographs using the Photo Bin. When you open one or more pictures in the Photo Editor, it shows up.

Among other things, the Photo Bin can be used to rotate photos, open and close photos, hide photos, and see file metadata.

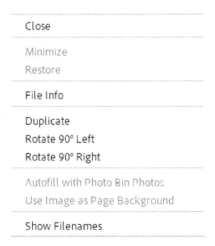

The **Menu Bar** is the collective name for the options located at the top of the workspace. Its constituent parts are File, Edit, Image, Enhance, Layer, Select, Filter, View, Window, and Help.

File   Edit   Image   Enhance   Layer   Select   Filter   View   Window   Help

The **Tool Panel** is a collection of tools available in the Photo Editor. The tools available in **Quick Mode** are fewer than the ones in **Advanced Mode** and are arranged into multiple groups or categories. The Tool Panel is located on the left-hand side of the Photo Editor.

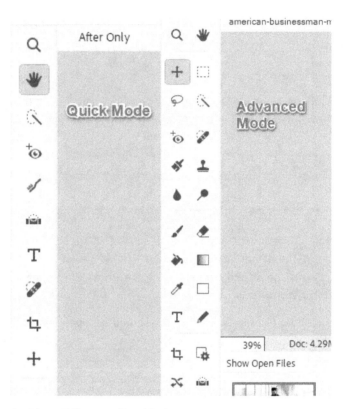

The tools available in the Photo Editor are listed below:

- **Zoom Tool**: The Zoom tool can be used to enlarge or reduce the view of a photograph.

The keyboard shortcut is **Z**

- **Hand Tool**: This is used in the Photoshop Element workspace to move pictures around. With this tool, you can also drag your image.

The keyboard shortcut is **H**

- **Move Tool**: In the Photo Editor, this tool is used to shift selections and layers.

The keyboard shortcut is **V**

- **Marquee Tools**: The two marquee tools available in Photoshop Elements are the ***Rectangular Marquee*** and the ***Ellipse Marquee*** tools. You can draw a rectangle box around a section of the image using the Rectangular Marquee Tool. Holding down the Shift key will cause the selection to become square.

The Ellipse Marquee tool is used to create an ellipse selection. Holding down the Shift key will make the selection into a circle.

The shortcut key for any of the Marquee Tools is **M**. Use **Shift + M** to toggle through any of them.

- **Lasso Tools**: The ordinary ***Lasso Tool*** (usually known as the Lasso Tool), ***Polygonal Lasso tool***, and ***Magnetic Lasso tool*** are the three categories of lasso tools.
  You can make a free-form selection in a particular region of the image by using the Lasso Tool.

When you choose a shape inside a picture, the Magnetic Lasso Tool helps to create a high-contrast outline. Like a magnet, it operates.

The polygonal lasso tool is used to create straight-edged selection border segments.

The keyboard shortcut for these tools is **L**. Use **Shift + L** to toggle through them.

- **Selection Tools**: Aside from the lasso tools and marquee tools, these tools are also used to make selections (select the part of a photograph). The keyboard shortcut key is **A**. Use **Shift + A** to toggle through the selection tools. The selection tools are listed below.
  Quick Selection Tool: Using this tool, selecting a color and texture will appear in any section of the image that is picked or dragged. This selecting tool responds to color.

Brush Selection Tool: You can choose the area you want to paint with the brush tool.

Magic Wand Tool: By doing this, a selection of clickable pixels with comparable colors is produced.

Refine Selection Brush: With this, you may add or remove a region from a selection while still having it automatically recognize the edges.

Auto Selection Tool: This automatically detects the edges of an area and can be used to add or remove it from a selection.

- **Rey Eye Tool**: This opens closed eyelids and gets rid of red-eye and pet-eye from your photos.

Keyboard Shortcut is **Y**

- **Spot Healing Brush Tool**: This is used to choose a section of an image and take out a stain.

Keyboard Shortcut is **J**

Healing Brush Tool: You can use the Healing Brush to remove flaws such as dust spots, wrinkles, and scratches so they blend in with the rest of the image.

Keyboard Shortcut is **J**

NB: The Spot Healing Brush Tool and the Healing Brush Tool are housed in the tool panel. You will find them separately in the Tool Options Panel. Use Shift+ J to toggle through them.

- **Smart Brush Tool**: This tool adjusts the tone and color balance of particular regions within an image.

Keyboard Shortcut is **F**

Detail Smart Brush Tool: This tool allows you to make adjustments as you paint certain portions of an image, just like the painting tool does.

Keyboard Shortcut is **F**

NB: The Smart Brush Tool and the Smart Brush Tool are housed in the tool panel. You will find them separately in the Tool Options Panel. Use Shift+ F to toggle through them.

- **Clone Stamp Tool**: Using an image sample, picture flaws, or just painting over items, you can use this tool to replicate objects, remove objects, or simply paint over parts in your image.

Keyboard Shortcut is **S**

Pattern Stamp Tool: This tool allows you to apply a pattern overlay on a photograph.

Keyboard Shortcut is **S**

NB: The Clone Stamp Tool and the Pattern Stamp Tool are housed in the tool panel. You will find them separately in the Tool Options Panel. Use Shift+ S to toggle through them.

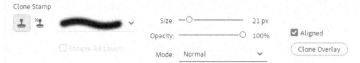

- **Blur Tool:** This is used to smooth down the rough spots and remove some of the edges.

Sharpen Tool: By concentrating on the soft edges of the image, this tool improves clarity and focus in pictures.

Smudge Tool: The instrument facilitates the smearing of wet paint with a brush. With this tool, you can drag the color from the stroke's starting point to the appropriate location.

NB: All three aforementioned tools are housed together and have their shortcuts to be **R.** Use Shift + R to toggle through the tools.

- **Sponge Tool**: This instrument stimulates a wet paint-smearing brush. This tool allows you to drag the color from the stroke's starting point to the desired location.

Dodge Tool: This is used on an image's lighter regions. With this tool, features in shadows can also be highlighted.

Burn Tool: This tool is used to add shadow to certain areas of an image. You can also use this tool to draw attention to particular details inside an image

The Keyboard shortcut for the sponge tool, dodge, and burn tool is **R**. You will find them separated in the Tool Options panel, use Shift + R to toggle through them.

- **Brush Tool**: This is employed to produce bold or subtle color strokes. It can also be used to improve retouching skills.

Impressionist Brush Tool: This is used to change the image's features and color.

Color Replacement Brush: With this tool, you can reduce the amount of a particular hue in your image.

NB: These brush tools have their keyboard shortcut to be **B.** Use Shift + B to toggle through them in the Tool Options Panel.

- **Eraser Tool**: As you move over the image, you can use this tool to decrease its pixel count. As you move over the image, you can use this tool to decrease its pixel count.

Background Eraser Tool: With this tool, you may easily erase an object from its background by altering a pixel's color to transparent.

Magic Eraser Tool: Using this tool, you can crop out a selection of pixels in an image that seems the same.

All eraser tools in the photo editor have their keyboard shortcut to be **E.** Use Shift + E to toggle through the eraser tools in the Tool Options Panel.

- **Paint Bucket Tool**: With the help of this tool, you can fill an area with a color value that nearly matches the pixels you've chosen or a pattern overlay to fill it up.

The keyboard shortcut is **K**

Available in the Tool Options Panel are the Color Fill and the Pattern Overlay options.

- **Gradient Tool**: Using this tool, you can add a gradient to a specific region of an image.

Keyboard Shortcut is **G**

- **Color Picker Tool**: This tool copies the color of a chosen portion of an image to create a new backdrop or foreground.

Keyboard Shortcut is **I**

- **Custom Shape Tool**: You may draw several forms with this tool.

Keyboard Shortcut is **U**

These forms are available in the Tool Options bar when the Custom Shape tool is selected. The Tool Options bar has the following shape tools: polygon, star, line, rectangle, ellipse, and selection.

- **Type Tool**: You can use this tool to add text to an image.

The keyboard Shortcut is **T**

Text on Shape, Text on Custom Path, Vertical Type, Horizontal Mask Type, and Vertical Type Mask are a few more type-related choices in the Tool Options bar.

- **Pencil Tool**: This tool is used to create strong-edged freehand lines on a photograph.

Keyboard Shortcut is **N**

- **Crop Tool**: This tool allows you to crop a certain portion of an image.

- **Cookie Cutter Tool**: With this tool, you can crop an image to any desired shape.

- **Perspective Crop Tool**: This tool is used to crop a photo while adjusting the viewpoint of the image.

NB: All these crop tools are housed together and separately displayed in the Tool Options Panel. Their Keyboard Shortcut is **C**.

- **Recompose Tool**: This allows for the clever resizing of photographs without sacrificing any of their qualities.

The keyboard shortcut is **W**

- **Content-Aware Move Tool**: This is the method for selecting an object and relocating it.

Keyboard Shortcut is **Q**

- **Straighten Tool**: An image can be moved vertically or horizontally with this.

Keyboard Shortcut is **P**

Located below the Tool panel are two color tabs overlapping each other; The Foreground and Background Color. They allow you to pick the color you want to apply with a tool on an image.

The **Tool Options Panel** is located at the bottom of the Image Window. One of the most useful workspaces for the Tools in Photoshop Elements is the Tool Options area. It provides several options that can be used with a certain tool. For instance, the Tool Options menu appears below when you click on the Crop Tool.

Using the Undo and Redo buttons, you can conduct an action again or return to a prior one respectively.

Rotate allows you to add the rotation effect to a picture or photo.

The *layout* allows you to rearrange your Image Windows in different styles using the images in the photo bin.

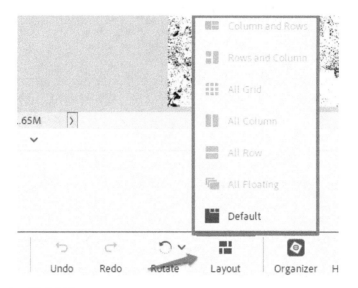

The image below is the **All Grid Layout**.

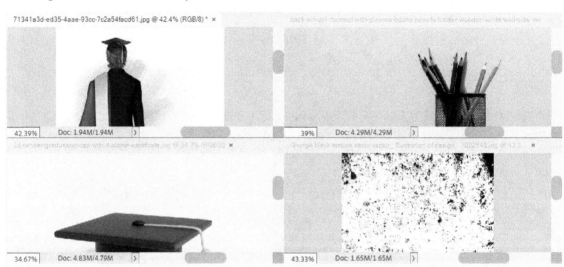

The **Organizer** icon leads you to the Organizer workspace while the **Home Screen** button takes you back to the interface of the Home Screen.

The panels are situated on the right side of the main screen in both the Quick and Advanced Edit modes. *Adjustments, Effects, Quick Actions, Textures*, and *Frames* are all included in the Quick Edit mode.

On the other hand, the Advanced edit mode has more panels, including *Styles, Graphics, Effects, Filters,* and *Layers*.

Keyboard Shortcuts in The Photo Editor
Listed below are shortcuts for using texts

RESULT	WINDOWS	MacOS
Drag and drop text within a picture	When the Type layer is selected, select the Control key and drag the type.	When the Type layer is selected, select the Command key and drag the type.
Modify the chosen text's font size by one point per point.	Control + Shift + < or >	Command + Shift + < or >
Activate or deactivate underlining.	Control + Shift + U	Command + Shift + U
Switch on or off Strikethrough.	Control + Shift + < or >	Command + Shift + < or >
Align left, center, or right	Horizontal Type or Horizontal Type Mask tool + Control + Shift + L, C, or R,	Horizontal Type or Horizontal Type Mask tool + Command + Shift + L, C, or R,
Align the top, center, or bottom	Control + Shift + L, C, or R + Vertical Type tool or Vertical Type Mask tool	Command + Shift + L, C, or R + Vertical Type tool or Vertical Type Mask tool
Choose a word, line, or passage.	Click twice, three times, or four times.	Click twice, three times, or four times

Here are several shortcuts for painting and brushing.

RESULT	WINDOWS	MacOS
To display the exact cross-hair on brushes.	Caps Lock	Caps Lock
To choose a background color.	Eyedropper tool + Alt-key	Eyedropper tool+ Opt-key
To apply background or foreground color to the selection or layer.	Control + Backspace or Alt-key + Backspace	Option + Delete or Command + Delete

Choose the first or last brush.	Shift +. (Period) or +, (Comma)	Shift + , (Comma) + . (Period)
To choose the prior/next brush size	. (Period) or, (Comma)	. (Period) or, (Comma)
To reduce or increase the brush size	[or]	[or]
To adjust the softness and hardness of the brush in increments of 25%.	Shift + [or]	Shift [or }
To remove brush	Alk-key + Brush	Option Key + Brush
To Use the Eyedropper Tool Instead	Any shape or painting tool + Alt- key (except Impressionist Brush)	Any shape or painting tool + Option Key (except Impressionist Brush)
To bring up the Fill dialog box	Shift + Backspace	Shift + Backspace
To paint with opacity, tolerance, or exposure set	Any painting or editing tool plus number keys (e.g., 0 Equals 100%, 1 = 10%, 4 and 5 quickly consecutively = 45%). To utilize the airbrush option, press the Shift + number keys.	A number key plus any painting or editing tool (e.g., 0 Equals 100%, 1 = 10%, 4 and 5 quickly consecutively = 45%). You can use the Shift + number keys to access the airbrush option.
Join points together by a straight line (draw a straight line)	Any painting tool + the Shift key	Any painting tool + the Shift key
Turn on/off the locking of transparent pixels	/ (forward slash)	/ (forward slash)
Turn the blending modes on and off.	Shift + + (plus) or - (minus)	Shift + + (plus) or - (minus)

Listed below are shortcuts for making selections

RESULT	WINDOWS	MacOS
Reflect or Transform from the center	Alt-Key	Option Key
Apply Transformation	Enter	Enter
Cancel Transformation	Control or Esc +. (Period)	Command or Esc +. (Period)
Constraint	Shift-Key	Shift-Key
Change Perspective	Control+ Shift+ Alt-Key	Command + Shift+ Option-Key
Distort	Control	Command
Skew	Control+ Shift	Command + Shift

The Organizer

The Organizer is a comprehensive component of Photo Elements, and it goes beyond the Photo Editor. It is utilized to maintain an effective and orderly collection of photographs, as its name suggests. In Photoshop Elements, it is also utilized for importing and navigating among photos.

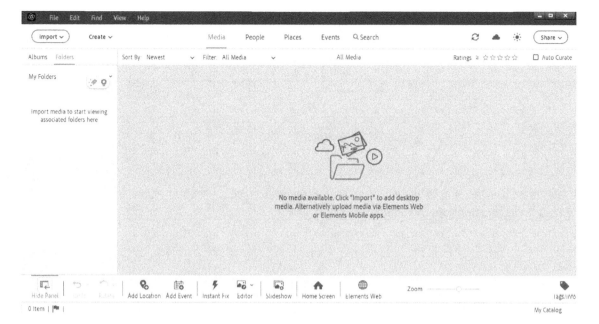

Navigating The Organizer

The **Menu Bar** contains the commands for carrying out operations or tasks in the Organizer. File. The commands File, Edit, Find, View, and Help Menu are available in the menu bar.

Using the **Import Button**, media files can be imported from files and directories, scanners, cameras, and card readers.

The **Create Button** allows you to work on multiple photo projects at once.

Album/Folder Tabs: All of your photo albums are located in your organizer's Album/Folder Tabs.

View Tabs: This section is divided into four categories: *Media, People, Places,* and *Events.* These categories let you find your pictures, photos, and files.

A list of every view tab in the Organizer may be seen below.

- **Media**: All of the media files are displayed or shown here. This window also allows you to modify your photo
- **People**: By utilizing the view tab, you can view photos based on the people in them (people). There is also an option to order the photos of the people who appear in them.
- **Places**: This display option allows you to view images categorized by the location or locations where they were taken. It's also possible to arrange the pictures according to the environment or place where they were taken.
- **Events**: You can construct an image-based stack of events in this view, with each event having an image. titling the photos from the event and include, say, a birthday celebration event.

You can use the **Search Button** to find photos and other media resources. To locate images or media, type a phrase in the Search drop-down menu.

Sort By allows you to order your media files in the organizer based on the names, batches, and most or least recent images that have been loaded or imported.

You can use the **Filter tool** to sort your media files according to All Media, Synched Media, or Local Media.

Ratings/Auto Curate: Your image or media item will be given a star rating using the rating tool. A rating system is an additional tool you may use to arrange and classify pictures and media items. With the help of the Auto Curator, you may use an image to automatically analyze and look for patterns.

Share: This is located on the far right side of the Home screen. You may make and share calendars, collages, and other things using this button.

Sync Icons: You can synchronize your media files to the cloud storage by using these two icons.

Features Button: This button has buttons for maximization, minimization, and closure. On Windows, these buttons are found in the upper-right area of the Organizer. Mac users will find these buttons on the left side.

Hide Panel: You can use this option to make the left panel of the Media Browser invisible so that you can see all of the photo thumbnails.

Undo/Rotate: This option allows you to rotate an image in both clockwise and counterclockwise directions. This is also where you can undo or redo an action by clicking on a small arrow.

Add Location: In the Organizer, you can add a new location in this section. Selecting this option causes the new location to be added to the Places panel and opens an Organizer window showcasing it.

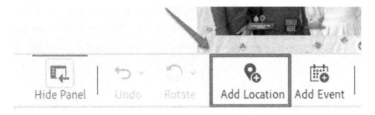

Add Event: This extra Organizer feature allows you to arrange pictures.

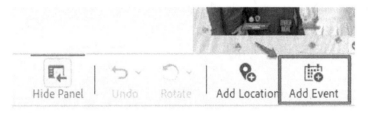

Instant Fix: Applying Quick Edit adjustments to your photographs is made simpler by using this tool. You may adjust lighting, crop, and fix red-eye with Instant Fix.

Editor: This icon allows you to return to the image editor.

Slideshow: Select the Slideshow button to launch the Memory project. The images are displayed as videos in the Slideshow.

Home Screen: Clicking this button takes you back to the Home screen.

Browse Web: This button takes you to Photoshop Elements' Beat version.

Thumbnail sizes can be changed by using the **Zoom function**.

Tag/Info: It is situated near the foot of the workplace, on the right. To access the Tag Panels, click on it. Tagging your images and media assets on the Organizer is one method of organizing them. Using tags to keep your photos organized is a great idea, and once your photos are categorized, managing them in the organizer is typically simpler.

The Preference Settings Dialog Interface

You can access the Preference dialog box by using either the Organizer or the Photo Editor.

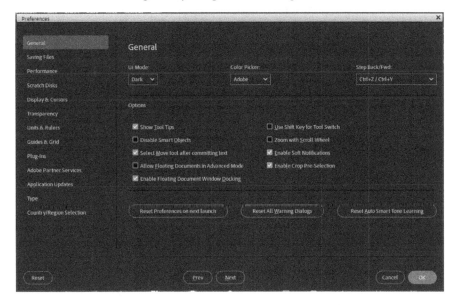

Photoshop Elements' tuning workshop is the Preference Dialog Box. This is the workspace where you can alter the software to suit your preferences.

You may adjust the UI mode, enable soft notifications, use the scroll wheel to control zoom, restore preferences, manage warning dialogs, and more under the General part of the Preferences dialog box. You can personalize your work and configure a program to fit your chosen working style with preference options. style and add something special to your work.

To access the preference settings via the Photo Editor/ Organizer, do the following.

- To open the Preference Dialog Box, select **Preference** from the **Edit Menu**, then click on any of the available options.

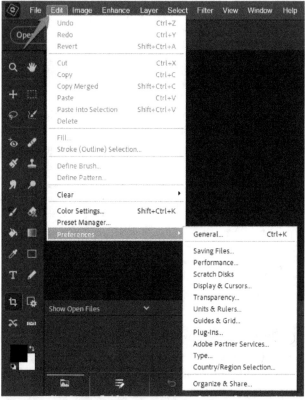

The Preference dialog box in the Photo Editor organizes the settings into panes for various Photoshop Element functions. When the Preference dialog box opens, the General pane is the first to show up.

Let's take a brief look at the functions and features of the Preference dialog box's control buttons.

- On the left side of the Preference dialog box is the Pane list, which displays various panels such as General, Saving files, Scratch disks, etc. Clicking on any of these pages will immediately expand your working possibilities. The preference panes are made up of many panes with different functionalities. Let us look more closely at each pane and its functions.

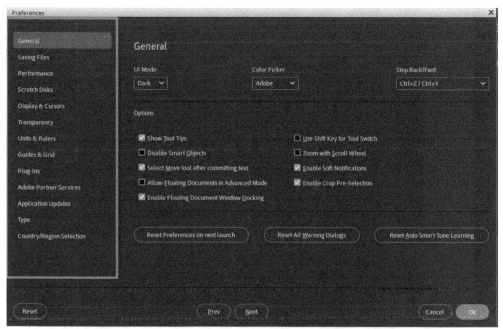

- **General:** This is where you adjust the general parameters of the editing environment.

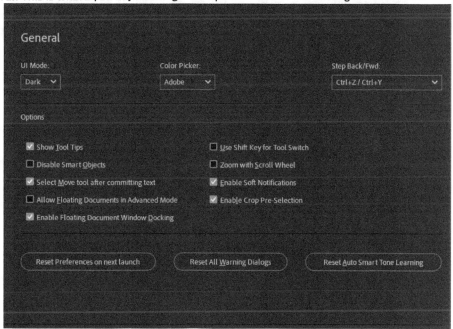

- **Saving Files:** You can add filename extensions and save files with picture previews, layers, and compatibility settings in this section.

- **Performance**: This is the window where historical data is shown along with memory parameters that regulate Photoshop Element's memory allocation.

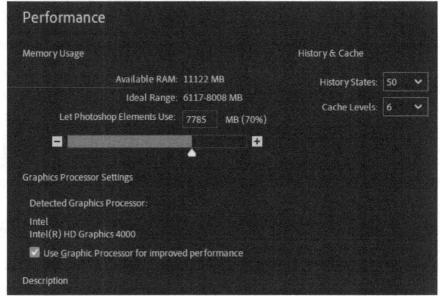

- **Scratch Disks**: This pane manages the use of the hard drive as an additional RAM extension.

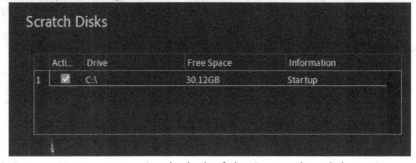

- **Display & Cursors**: You can customize the look of the Crop tools and the various tool cursors while cropping photos in these panels.

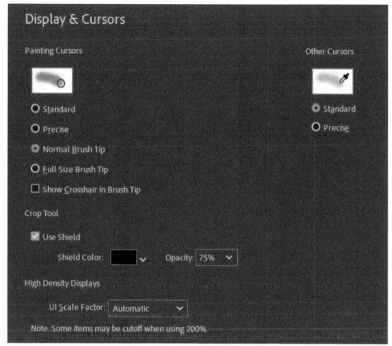

- **Transparency**: Using this, you may select how the element in these panes will display transparency.

- **Units & Rulers**: In this way, you can establish the default resolutions for the document, the column guide, and the ruler units.

- **Guides & Grid**: This provides features for color, divisions, and subdivision of the gridline.

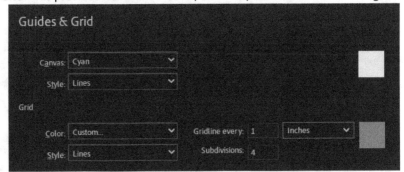

- **Plug-Ins**: This takes care of selecting an additional Plug-Ins folder. Plug-ins, or third-party applications, enable you to accomplish tasks that Element does not cover. The Photoshop Element Plug-Ins can be found online.

- **Adobe Partner Services**: Elements can now reset all account information, look for new services, and remove any data stored online. These allow you to configure the Element application to get updates automatically and to be informed when a new version is made available.

- **Application Updates**: You can change how your program responds to new Adobe updates by using this pane.

- **Type**: This is where you change the text attributes of the setting. You can test font sizes in addition to using font kinds like Asian characters that show the font name in English.

- **Country/Region Selection**: Selecting a country or region allows you to make a selection from a list of possibilities.

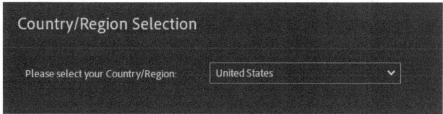

- **Reset**: This option returns the original settings of the Preference dialog box. After resetting, the dialog box where you modify the new options stays open.
- **Prev**: Press this button to return to the previous pane.
- **Next**: Press this button to move to the following pane.
- **Cancel**: Pressing this button finally closes the dialog box and restores the page to its original configuration.

CHAPTER THREE

HOW TO USE THE ORGANIZER

Maximizing The Organizer for Effective Use

Using Tags

Tags are one technique to help you keep your media files and photos organized on the Organizer. Using tags is a great way to keep your photos organized, and once they are categorized, managing them in the organizer is typically simpler. Analysis and categorization can be performed using an image's time of capture, among other things.

Do the following to create tags.

- Click on Your Media Browser, then select the images you wish to tag with labels.

- Select **Tag/Info** at the lower right-hand side of the organizer's interface.

- Click on the plus sign (New button) to add a new tag.

- In the Name text field, type the tag's name, then choose an icon from the Category Icon.

- Next, click OK.

To add icons to a tag, do the following.

- Navigate to the tag you want to edit in the Tag section.

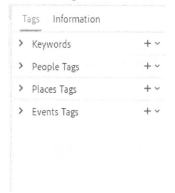

- Right-click the tag you want to edit and select **Edit**.

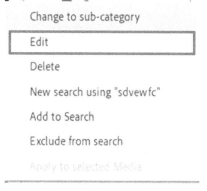

- Choose "**Edit Icon**."

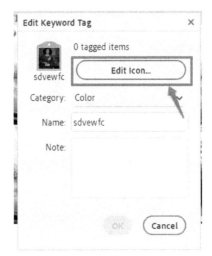

- To find the picture that should be used as the icon, browse through the folder by clicking the **Import button** in the **Edit Keyword Tag Icon** dialog box.

- After selecting your favorite photo, click **Open.**

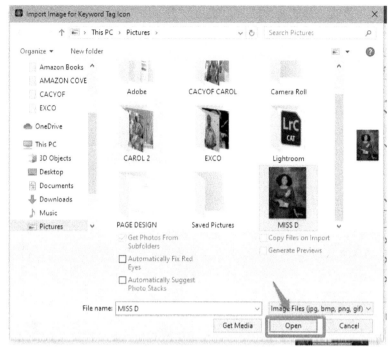

- Then hit the "OK" button.

Importing Images

The Organizer allows you to upload photographs in two main ways. You can utilize the File Menu's "Get Photos and Videos" option or the Import button.

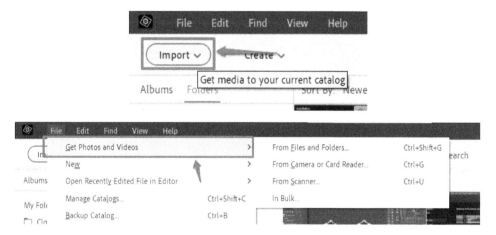

There are several ways to import images into the organizer and we will be learning them in this section.

To import from Files And Folders, go to the guidelines provided below.

- Select the File menu in the Organizer, and click on Get Photo and Videos.

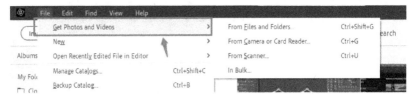

- Select From **Files and Folders**.

- From your hard drive, select the image or folder you want to import and select **Get Media.**

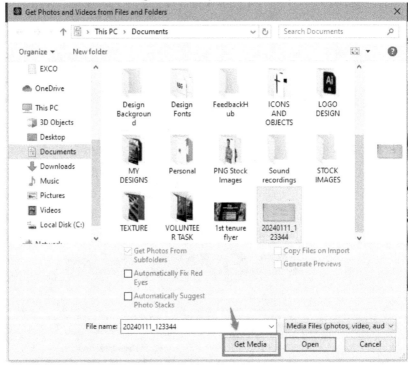

To import images from a camera, do the following.

- You can use a USB connector to connect the media card to your computer or insert the card directly from the camera to view the organizer window.
- From the File menu, choose "**Get Photo and Videos.**" Next, select "**From Camera or Card Reader.**"

- Select the media card using the drop-down list in the Adobe Photo Downloader dialog box's Get Photos From section.

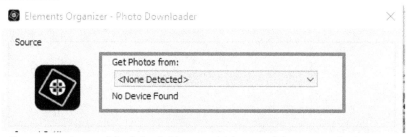

- Choose the Browse option and find the folder to which you wish to copy the image.

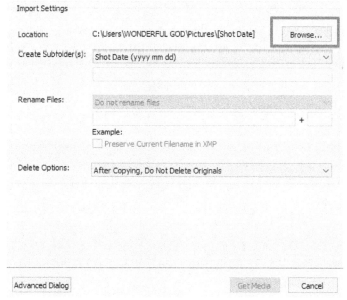

- Click the Get Media option to import the photographs after checking the importation settings.

To import from a scanner, follow the instructions below.

- From the File menu, choose "**Get Photo and Videos**," and then select "**From Scanner**."

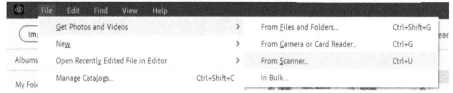

- In the Get **Photos From Scanner** dialog box, choose the scanner that you are importing from.

- To choose the location where the files you are importing will be imported, click **Browse**.

- At Save As, choose the format in which you wish to store your photos.

- To assess the quality of your photos, use the Quality Slider.

- When you're ready to import the photos, click OK.
- After making all the required adjustments to the scanned image, click the Scan button in the resulting dialog box.

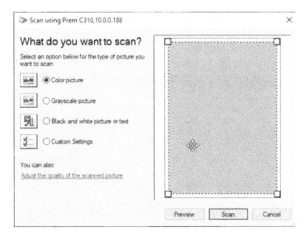

Follow these steps to import in bulk.

- Click on In Bulk after selecting Get Photo and Videos from the File menu.

- Make sure the folders you want to import from are ticked/checked.

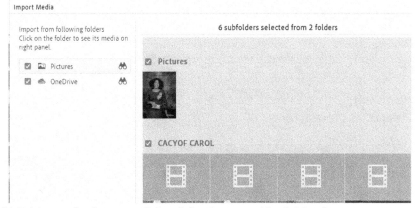

- Select **Add Folder** at the bottom of the dialog box to add a folder from your computer to the organizer.

- Select **Import** to upload the images to the Organizer.

Here are the steps to import your phone's images into your organizer.

- Use a USB cord to connect the devices.
- Choose **Get Photos and Videos** from File by going to File, then click **From Files and Folder**.

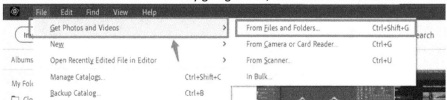

- Navigate through the folder where you copied the file on the device before moving on to the organizer.

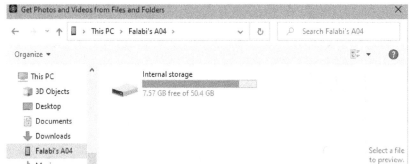

- To finish importing the photographs into the organizer, select the ones you wish to import and then click **Get Media**.

Working with Albums

To make an album, do these steps.

- Select the photos you wish to have in the album.

- Choose **Album** from the Organizer's left-hand menu.

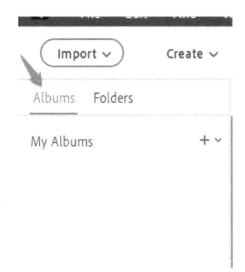

- Click the plus (+) icon and choose **New Album**.

- Enter the name of the album in the Name text field in the right-hand panel and choose the album's category from the drop-down menu.

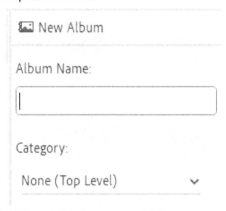

- When you're finished, click **OK**, and the images ought to appear on the Media browser's left side.

To add photos to an album, you can do any of the following:

- To build the album, drag and drop the pictures from the Media view into the Album panel.
- From the Album panel, drag the album to the image in the Media view.

- You may also select the stack and drag it into the album.

To make an album category, take the following actions.

- Choose **Album** from the Organizer's left-hand menu.

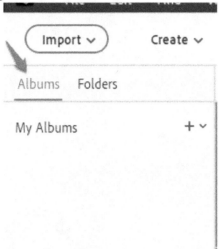

- Click the downward arrow next to the plus (+) symbol and select the **New Album Category** option.

- In the Name text box and Category drop-down menu located on the right side of the panel, respectively, type the album's name and category.

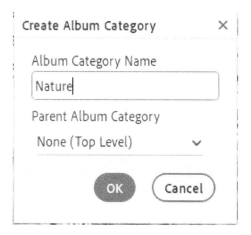

- Next, click **OK**.

To remove a photograph from an album, follow the steps outlined below.

- To remove a picture from the album, pick the picture with a right-click, then choose **Remove From Album.**

The following guidelines can be utilized to remove an album from the Album panel:

- Select **Delete** after doing a right-click on the album.

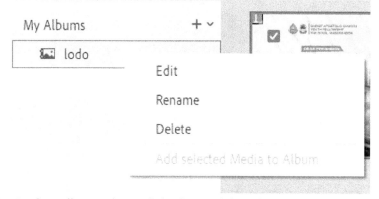

- Click OK in the Confirm Album Deletion dialog box to delete the album.

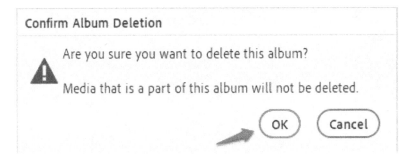

Confirm Album Deletion

Are you sure you want to delete this album?

Media that is a part of this album will not be deleted.

OK   Cancel

You can use album sorting, reverse chronological, or chronological organizing methods to arrange the photos in your album. You can use the following procedures to organize the pictures in an album.

- Select an album from the **Album** and **Folders** panel.

- Choose any pick from the following choices in the Media view's **Sort By** drop-down menu.

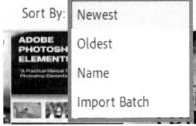

✦ **Newest**: Using this option, the images are arranged chronologically, starting with the most recent.
✦ **Oldest**: This collection's images are arranged chronologically from oldest to newest.
✦ **Name**: This option arranges the content alphabetically from A to Z.
✦ **Impact Batch**: When this option is selected, the photos are arranged according to the date of import into batches.

Working with Catalogues
It's as easy as pie to launch or open a catalog; just follow the steps listed below.

- From the File menu, find Manage Catalogs and select it.

- In the Catalog Manager dialog box, click the catalog you want to open.

- Choose **Open** after that.

To make a catalog, take the following actions.

- From the **File menu**, find **Manage Catalogs** and select it.

- In the Catalog Manager dialog box, select **New**.

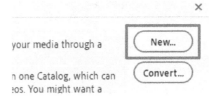

- Enter the new catalog's name in the File Name text field, then click **OK**.

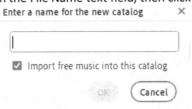

Do the following to add images/photographs to your freshly formed catalog.

- Choose the **Get Photos and Videos** option from the **File Menu**.

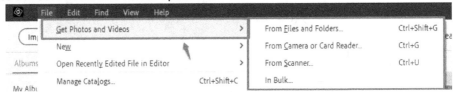

- Choose the desired photos from the Get Photo and Videos dialog box, then click **Get Media** to import the images.

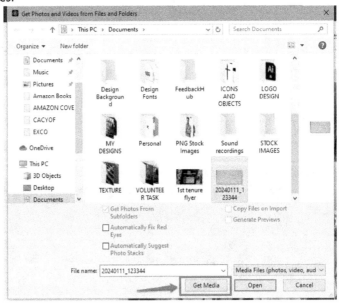

The actions mentioned below can be taken to back up your catalog:

- Use **Ctrl + B** or choose **Backup Catalog** from the File Menu.

- Click the Next button after choosing an option from the list below to see the Backup Catalog dialog box.

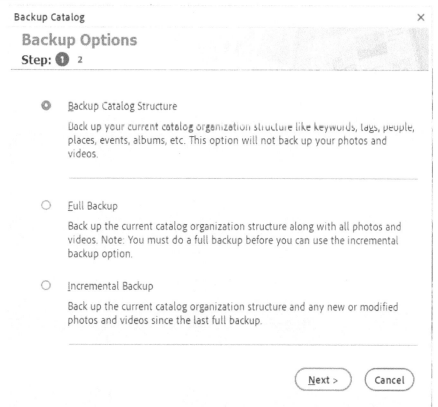

- ✦ **Backup Catalog Structure**: This option allows you to create a backup of the entire structure of your catalog, including its tags, users, locations, and events. In this instance, the images and videos are not in the backup.
- ✦ **Full Backup**: When creating your initial backup or writing files to a new media source, this choice is chosen. In a nutshell, this option backs up everything in your collection, including the images and photos.
- ✦ **Increment Backup**: When you've completed at least one backup and want to update the files you've backed up, you select this option.
- To choose the **Destination Drive** on the next page, click the drive letter of your choice.

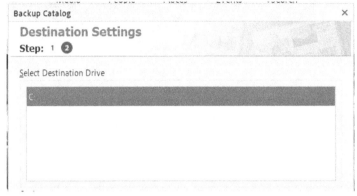

- Use **Browse** to locate the backup catalog's storage location.

- Finally, use the **Save Backup button** by clicking on it to finish the backup.

The procedures listed below can be used to make a backup of your images and files:

- Go to the **File menu** and select **Copy/Move to Removable**.

- When the subsequent dialog box appears, click **Yes.**

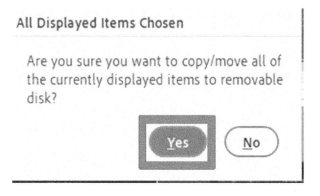

- In the dialog box that displays, click **Copy Files**, and then select **Next**.

- Click **Done** once you've selected a hard disk and typed the name of the backup folder.

To restore a backed-up catalog, follow these steps.

- Navigate to **File** and choose **Restore Catalog** to open the Restore Catalog.

- From the **Restore From** dialog box, **CD/DVD, Hard Drive/Other Volume** should be selected from the dialog box that displays.

- Click **Browse** to find the hard disk if that's where you stored your backup.

- After selecting the backup file, select the location for the backup file's restoration by clicking Browse in the Restore To dialog box.

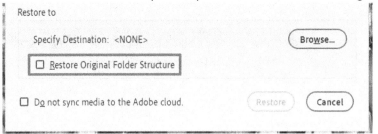

- **Restore Original Folder Structure** is the option to preserve the files in the catalog.

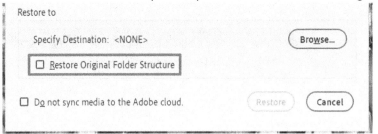

- Press the **Restore** button after that.

Auto-Curate, Auto creation, and Ranking
Auto Curating is one of the fundamental features of the organizer that I will be introducing to you in this section.

When searching through photos, the Auto Curator looks for visual resemblance. When the tests are complete, the top photos show up in the Media Browser. To perform this operation, at least ten photos are required.

The *Auto Curator* check box is located in the upper-right area of the Organizer pane.

Auto Creation?

To make the most out of Auto Creation, which you may use to create a range of effects in your photos, you should familiarize yourself with it.

- From the Edit Menu, select Preference

- Select **Media Analysis**, and then click on **Generate Auto Creations** to enable Auto Creation.

Ranking??

Users can rate photos in the Organizer by giving them a star rating between one and five. Five stars is the greatest rating, and one star is the lowest. You also can organize your pictures according to ratings. To assign a star to a photograph, do the following.

- Choosing the image with the Media Browser.
- Use the "**Ratings**" tab on the right side of the screen and choose one or two stars to rate anything.

Adding Events

Through your Media Browser, you can add a new event. Just follow these steps to make this happen.

- In the lower-left corner of the organizer, click Add New Event.

- Click Done after entering the name, start date, end date, and description exactly as they appear in the dialogue window.

Add New Event

Name: Graduating

Start Date: 1/3/2024

End Date: 1/3/2024

Group: None

Description:

1 Item

Done   Cancel

CHAPTER FOUR

NECESSARY OPERATIONS TO KNOW TO MASTER PHOTOSHOP ELEMENTS

Fundamentals in Photoshop Elements 2024

You have two options when starting a new document: either open an already-existing picture or photo in your photo editor or start from scratch and make a blank canvas that you may use to draw whatever kind of design you require.

Creating A New Document

To start a new design document in Photoshop Elements, follow these steps.

- Choose **New** from the **File Menu**, then click **Blank File** or press the **Ctrl + N** shortcut.

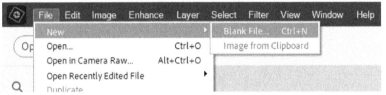

- The dialog box for creating a new document opens.

- Enter the new file's name in the **Name Bar**.

- In **Document Type**, specify the type of document.

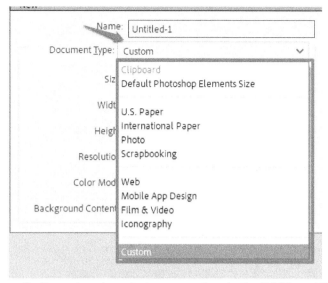

- Change the document's dimensions by entering new values in the **Width** and **Height** boxes.

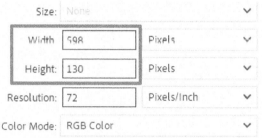

- You may adjust the unit of measurement by clicking on the downward arrow next to Pixels.

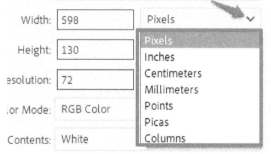

- Add more figures to the **Resolution** bar to change the resultant document's quality.

- Toggle the **Color Mode** bar to change the new document's color mode.

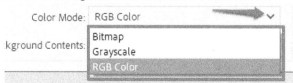

- To choose the appearance of your canvas, use **Background Content**.

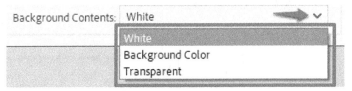

- To store your changed settings on the system for easy access the next time, use **Save Preset**.

- Click **OK** to start the new document after making the necessary changes to its settings.

- After clicking on **OK**, the image Window displays the created document.

Opening A Photograph/Image

To open a photograph, do the following.

- Open the **Photo Editor**.

- Either choose **Open** from the **File Menu** or click the **Open button**.

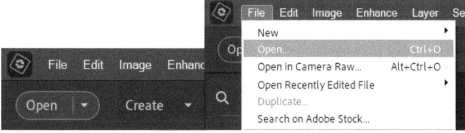

- Click on **Open** after selecting your preferred image from the **Open Dialog box**.

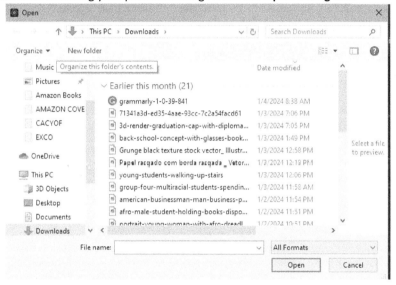

To open a photo in Camera Raw, follow these steps.

- Click on **File** and then choose **Open in Camera Raw**.

- Photoshop Elements prompts you to download the Camera Raw plugin if you don't already have it installed on your computer.

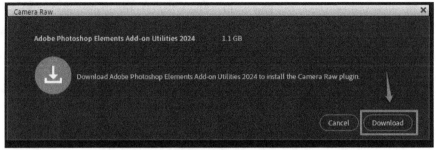

- To install the Plugin, select **Download**.
- To install the Camera Raw Plug-in, go to the on-screen instructions that follow.
- After installation, the Camera Raw appears.

To view recently edited files, take the following actions.

- Choose **Recently Edited Files** from the **File Menu**, then click on the file you want to access again.

- A list of recently opened files is displayed.

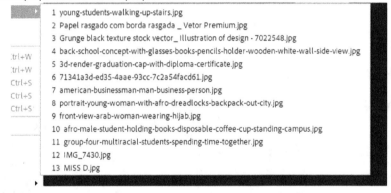

Importing Photographs

In Photoshop Elements, you can add a photograph/image to a project design you are working on by doing the following.

- Click on **Place** after selecting the **File Menu**. You'll reach your File Manager as a result.

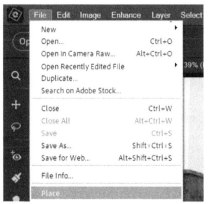

- Click **Place** after selecting a picture.

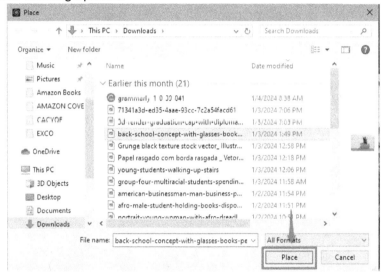

- To apply the size modification, resize the imported file to the desired size and click the done icon.

ATTENTION! ATTENTION!! ATTENTION!!!

Have you read Todd Lemming`s first book on Photoshop Elements 2024??

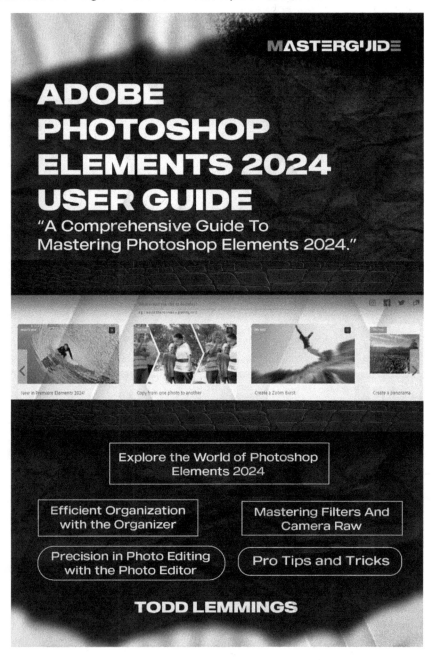

Have you ever experienced the frustration of not knowing where to begin when using picture editing software? What if you could solve the puzzles of Photoshop Elements 2024 and accurately and easily alter your photos?

Are your photos missing that professional touch?
Do you dream of transforming ordinary images into extraordinary works of art?
Dive into "Photoshop Elements 2024 User Guide" and discover the secrets to unlocking the full potential of your creative vision.

Then this book is for you!!!

Make the most of your photo-editing experience by using this "Photoshop Elements 2024 User Guide" to its fullest. Your key to grasping Photoshop Elements 2024's most recent capabilities is this meticulously written book, which is appropriate for novices as well as seasoned users.

Discover the World of Photoshop Elements 2024:
Uncover the fundamentals with a perceptive overview of Photoshop Elements 2024, dispelling any confusion regarding its features and user interface. This book offers a strong basis for self-assured navigation, regardless of experience level.

Efficient Organization with the Organizer:
Discover how to use the organizer's power to streamline your creative process. Effortlessly organize, classify, and arrange your images to improve productivity and maintain a spotless digital workspace.

Precision in Photo Editing with the Photo Editor:
Utilize the Photo Editor module to unleash your artistic side. This book walks you through every stage, from simple tweaks to sophisticated methods. With thorough instructions and practical examples, you can turn average images into exceptional pieces of art.

Mastering Filters and Camera Raw:
Become an expert editor by delving deeply into Camera Raw and Filters. Investigate a wide range of artistic possibilities to improve and style your photos. This part gives you the ability to express your perspective by revealing the techniques behind editing at the professional level.

Pro Tips and Tricks:
Learn the insider strategies and tricks used by pros to accomplish amazing outcomes. You'll find a wealth of information in this section that will elevate your experience with Photoshop Elements 2024, from sophisticated methods to time-saving shortcuts.

What You Will Find
- Inside are comprehensive courses suitable for both novice and expert users.
- Useful illustrations to support your knowledge.
- Detailed instructions for effective photo management.
- Innovative methods for powerful picture manipulation.
- insider knowledge to make editing smooth and easy.

Take a trip through time-traveling magic with "Photoshop Elements 2024 User Guide." Learn the techniques for effective planning, accurate editing, and artistic expression, and see how your pictures come to life like never before. This book is your key to maximizing Photoshop Elements 2024's capabilities, regardless of your level of experience.

CHAPTER FIVE

SAVING AND EXPORTING FILE

Saving Files/Projects

In Photoshop Elements, there are three commands for saving projects, designs, and images: **Save, Save As, and Save For Web**.

Save	Ctrl+S
Save As...	Shift+Ctrl+S
Save for Web...	Alt+Shift+Ctrl+S

Save Command

To save the changes made to the file being worked on, use the **Save command**. You can perform either of the following to make this happen.

- Click on Save after opening the file and choosing File Menu.

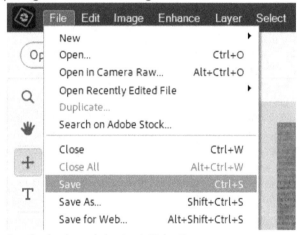

- Alternatively, save using the keyboard shortcut **Ctrl + S**.

Save As Command

When saving photos, you can adjust several aspects such as the file name, file type, layers, and more using the **Save As** option.

Follow these steps to save files using the Save As Command.

- Select the image that you wish to save as a file when Photoshop Element opens.
- As soon as the File Menu displays, select Save As.

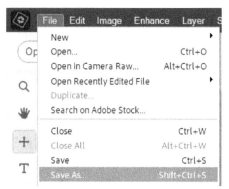

- In the File Name text area, enter the file's name and select the location for storage.

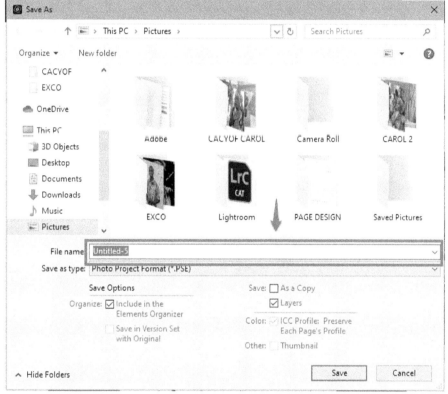

- Click the File Format option to select the format that you want the file to be stored in (Options available are dependent on the type of project you`re trying to save.)

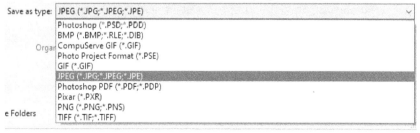

- Additional capabilities are available to use with the Save As command under the Save Options.

❖ If you select the "**Include In the Elements Organizer**" option, the saved file will be shown in the Photo Browser and added to the library. Several file formats, most notably the EPS file format, do not support the Element organizer.

```
Save Options                        Save: ☐ As a Copy
┌──────────────────────────────┐           ☐ Layers
│ Organize: ☑ Include in the   │
│            Elements Organizer │    Color: ☑ ICC Profile:  sRGB
└──────────────────────────────┘    Other: ☑ Thumbnail
           ☐ Save in Version Set
              with Original
```

❖ **Save In Version Set with** Original: This option preserves several iterations of the image by saving the file and adding it to a version set in the Photo Browser. You can only utilize this option after choosing **Include In the Organizer**.

```
Save Options                        Save: ☐ As a Copy
Organize: ☑ Include in the                ☐ Layers
           Elements Organizer
                                    Color: ☑ ICC Profile:  sRGB
┌──────────────────────────────┐    Other: ☑ Thumbnail
│        ☐ Save in Version Set  │
│           with Original       │
└──────────────────────────────┘
```

❖ **Save As a Copy**: When this choice is made, the open file is saved as a copy. The folder where the open file is located is where the file copy is saved.

```
Save Options                   ┌─────────────────────┐
                               │ Save: ☐ As a Copy   │
Organize: ☑ Include in the     └─────────────────────┘
           Elements Organizer         ☐ Layers
                                Color: ☑ ICC Profile:  sRGB
           ☐ Save in Version Set Other: ☑ Thumbnail
              with Original
```

❖ **Save As Layers**: Using this option improves the image's layer retention. When the Layer option is disabled or inaccessible, the image has no layers. A warning icon appears in the Layer check box when the image's layer needs to be merged or flattened for the chosen format. Choose a different format if you want to keep the layers in an image intact.

```
Save Options                        Save: ☐ As a Copy
                               ┌─────────────────────┐
Organize: ☑ Include in the     │        ☐ Layers     │
           Elements Organizer  └─────────────────────┘
                                Color: ☑ ICC Profile:  sRGB
           ☐ Save in Version Set Other: ☑ Thumbnail
              with Original
```

❖ **ICC Profile**: This indicates that you can apply a color profile to the image in certain formats.

```
Save Options                        Save: ☐ As a Copy
Organize: ☑ Include in the                ☐ Layers
           Elements Organizer  ┌────────────────────────────┐
           ☐ Save in Version Set│ Color: ☑ ICC Profile:  sRGB│
              with Original     └────────────────────────────┘
                                Other: ☑ Thumbnail
```

❖ **Thumbnails**: This option stores details about the thumbnail of the file. When the Preferences dialog box's Ask When Saving for Image Preview option is activated, this option becomes available.

```
Save Options                        Save: ☐ As a Copy
Organize: ☑ Include in the                ☐ Layers
           Elements Organizer
                                    Color: ☑ ICC Profile:  sRGB
           ☐ Save in Version Set ┌─────────────────────┐
              with Original      │ Other: ☑ Thumbnail  │
                                 └─────────────────────┘
```

Save For Web

You can adjust photos for usage on web-based media (the Internet), such as blogs and webpages, by altering the display properties and compressing them using the **Save For Web** command. Nonetheless, the three most popular file types on the internet are GIF, JPEG, and PNG.

To utilize Save For Web, follow the steps indicated below.

- Choose Save For Web from the File Menu.

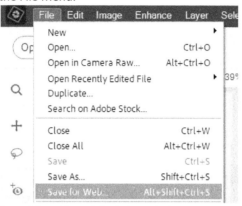

- This brings up the many optioned Save For Web dialog window.

- Use the tools in the Tool Bar to edit your project.
  - **Hand Tool**: When zoomed in, use this tool to move around the image in the Preview section.
  - **Zoom Tool**: This tool lets you adjust the size of the preview image.
  - **Eyedropper Tool**: This tool lets you see a color in an image exactly as it appears in the Preview area. This is a preview of how the image will look.

❖ **The Windows for Preview**: following its storage. The preview is shown in the second image, while the actual image is shown in the first.

Original: "young-students-walking-up-stairs.jpg"
4.29M

GIF
816.4K
149 sec @ 56.6 Kbps

100% dither
Selective palette
256 colors

❖ **Presets**: Using this option, you can choose from a number of the drop-down menu's presets. The preset is used to establish pre-configured settings for the dialog box's options.

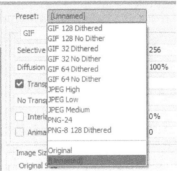

❖ **Image Format**: A drop-down menu allows you to choose a file format here (GIF, JPEG, or PNG).

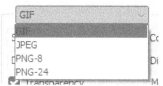

♦ **Quality Settings**: Before saving the shot, this is where you change its quality. The Quality option appears when you save any file as a JPEG; for GIF and PNG, you can adjust the color number.

♦ **Image Attributes**: This selection's Original Size section shows the original width and height. In the New Size Area, you can change the image's width and height as percentages or as pixels.

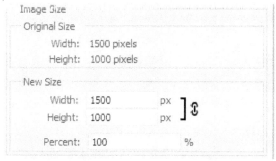

♦ **Animation**: This option is only applicable to animated GIFs.

♦ **Menu Preview**: An excerpt of the final product is available here.

Sharing Projects/Files

Photoshop Elements offers two options for sharing media files: the Organizer and the Photo Editor.

Sharing Via Photo Editor

Follow these steps to use Photo Editor to share photographs on many platforms.

- Open the Photo Editor from the Home Screen.

- When the Photo Editor opens, select the picture you wish to share.
- Click **Share** after selecting a choice from the Share drop-down menu.

Sharing Via Organizer

To use the Organizer to share photographs, follow the guidelines below.

- Open the Organizer by going to the Home Screen.

- Select the picture you want to share and then select Media from the Organizer.
- Click to bring up the **Share** drop-down menu, then select an item.

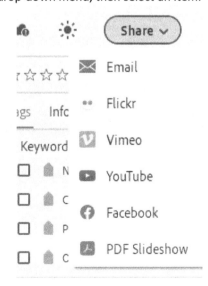

Printing Photographs

With Photoshop Elements, you have total control over photo printing. It is possible to print contact sheets, photo packages, and pictures.

To print any of your completed products, follow these steps.

- Use the keyboard shortcut **Ctrl/Cmd + P** to print, or choose **Print** from the **File Menu**.

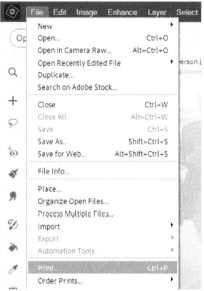

- In the Print dialog box, you can preview the print and change its parameters.

- Choose **Select Printer** to choose the printing type from the drop-down list.

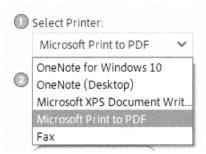

- **Printer Settings** display the printing process's current settings.

To change the printer's settings, select **Change Settings**. Use the Printer Settings to set up the printer, paper size, paper type, paper tray, and print quality.

- **Select Paper Size**: Select the paper size you wish to print photos on from the drop-down list.

- **Orientation**: Select whether the page should be viewed in landscape or portrait orientation.

- **Select Print Type**: Contact sheet, picture package, and individual prints are the print options that are offered here.

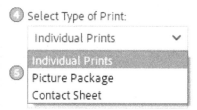

- **Select Print Size**: You should decide on the print size for the photo. Click Custom to adjust the photo's proportions. For more details, go to the Scale pictures.

- **Crop To Fit**: Use this tool to make an image fit into a specific print arrangement. The image is cropped and adjusted as necessary to meet the aspect ratio of the print arrangement. Click this button to deselect the cropping of your images.

- **Print**: You can either put the desired number into the text box or choose the desired number to indicate how many copies of each page you want to print.

Print 1 copies

- **Photos Selected for Printing** and **Add Photos for Printing appear** on the left side of the dialog box.

- You can check out the lower part of the left workspace for other options and commands.

- Once the settings are adjusted, choose **Print** to get your pictures printed.

CHAPTER SIX
PHOTO PROJECTS CREATION

Working With Photo Projects

By combining two or more photographs in any format of your choosing, you may create photo projects using the **Create button**, including Slideshows, Photo Collages, Photo Reels, Quote Graphics, Photo Prints, Photo Books, Greeting Cards, and Photo Calendars.

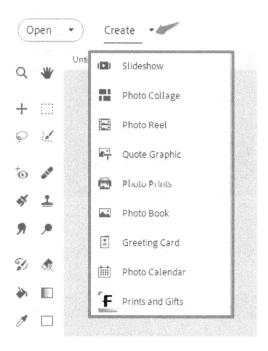

The format in which picture projects are saved is called the Photo Projects Format (.pse). You can print the picture projects from your home printer, save them to your hard drive, or send them via email.

Creating A Slideshow
- Select **Create** and click on **Slideshow**.

- Select **OK** when the interface below pops up on your screen and the Organizer interface will be opened up to you.

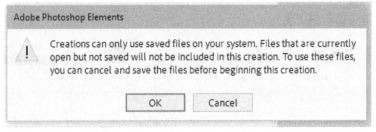

- In the media grid, choose the pictures and videos you want.

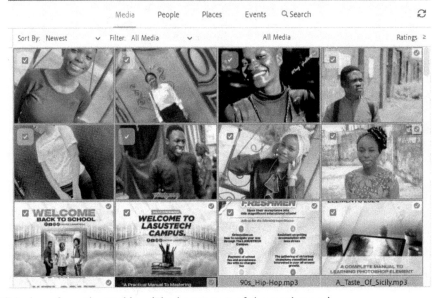

- Select **Slideshow** from the **Taskbar** (The lower part of the workspace).

- Using the chosen media files, a slideshow preview is created in the Slideshow window.

- Click **Add Captions** in the top-right corner of the Media box to add a caption to each picture.

- Click to add a text slide, then type the title and subtitle, then click Add.

Title: Enter Title

Subtitle: Enter Subtitle

Cancel   Add

- To add more photos and videos to the slideshow click on **Add Photos and Videos** and select the method selection from the drop-down menu.

- Select **Media** to make changes to each picture or video in the slideshow and view the chosen media files.

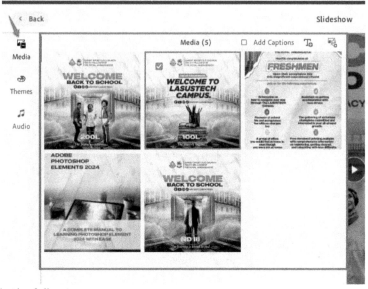

You can also do the following.

- ○ Drag and drop the desired media file arrangement onto the desired media file selection to modify its order.
- ○ In the Media panel, you can flip or erase a picture. Right-click a picture and choose the desired option from the drop-down list to accomplish this.

- ○ Right-click on a video file to trim the Video, and mute and unmute the audio track.

- • Change the theme and the transition style of the slideshow in the **Theme** section.

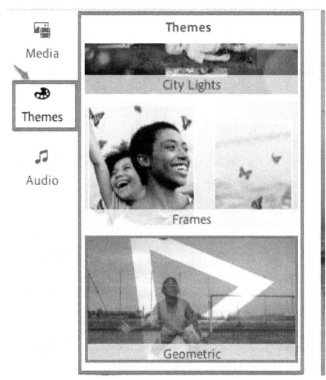

- Select **Audio** to change the background song in the slideshow.

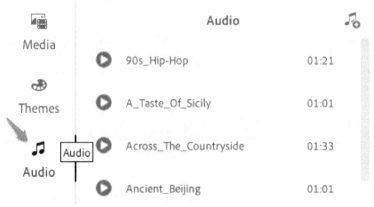

- Click **Save** to save the slideshow to the organizer.

- After making the necessary edits, select **Export** to export a slideshow to your hard drive.

Creating A Photo Collage

To make a photo collage, do the following.

- Select two or more images from the Photo bins once Photoshop Elements has opened. You may choose a minimum of eight pictures to use in a collage.

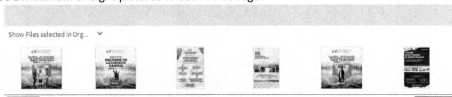

- Select **Photo Collage** after selecting **Create**.

- A smart auto-crop creates a picture collage, the collage frames are automatically produced based on the number of open photos, and the most conspicuous aspect of the shot (the face) is selected and placed in them.

- You can add more photos to your photo collage by choosing Computer or Organizer in the Add Photos From dialog box (on the right side of the workspace).

- Select a **layout** for your photo collage on the workspace's right side.

- To select a background or frame, click **Graphics** in the lower-right corner of the screen. Double click the selection to include it in your collage.

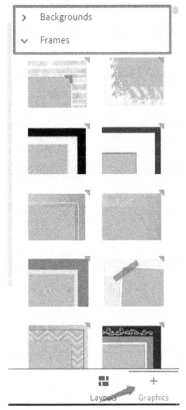

- All you need to do is right-click on an image if you want to edit it and carry out common operations like *Rotate 90 Right, Rotate 90 Left, Drag to Swap Photo, Change Background, Replace Photo*, and *Remove Photo*.

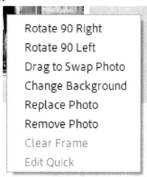

Creating Photo Reels

To make a picture reel, do these steps.

- Once you've chosen two or more photos, click Create and choose Photo Reel.

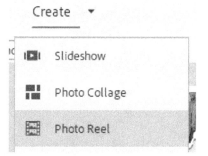

- You can add more images and movies to your photo reel by choosing Computer or Organizer in the Add Media From dialog box (on the workspace's right side).

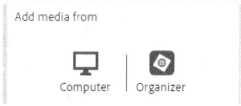

- *The Zoom Tool, Hand Tool, Move Tool,* and *Text Tool* are the available tools in the Photo Reel workspace. Either of these can be used to modify your project.

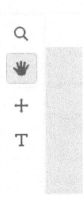

- To examine and modify the length of each picture in the photo reel, click **Timeline**.

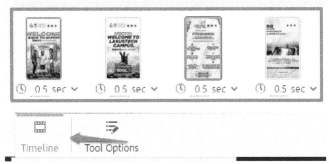

- Press the descending arrow to change how long each picture lasts.

- To modify the layout size of your photo, select **Layout** from the workspace's right side.

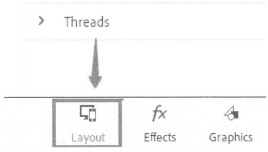

- To apply effects to each media, select the options located under **Effects** on the workspace's right side.

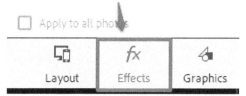

- To apply a single effect to every photo in your photo reel, select **Apply to All Photos**. You can then play about with the **Intensity Slider** to change how strong the effects are on each shot.

- To incorporate clip art and emoticons into your pictures, choose design components from **Graphics**.

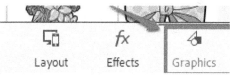

- To save your photo reel, click **Export**.

Creating Quote Graphics
To make a quote graphic, do the following steps.

- Choose **Create** first, then select **Quote Graphics**.

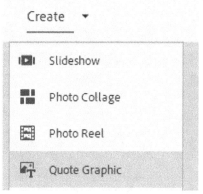

- You have three options from the dialog box: **Choose from The Pre-Existing Template, Start from Scratch**, or **Start With A Photo**.

- Select template size.

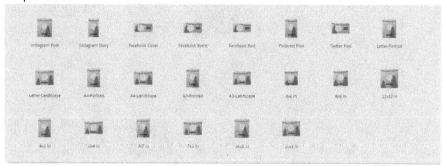

- Use any of the available options in **Add Photos From**, which are located on the workspace's right, to add more photos to your projects.

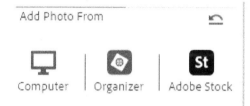

- Select any desired background overlay from the **Background Panel**.

- To add test styles, update texts, add texts, and adjust text size, select the **Text Panel**.

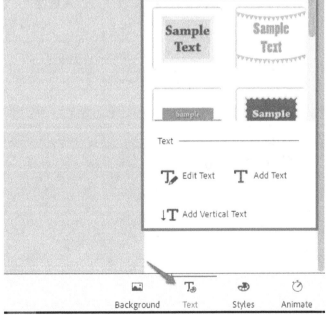

Using the Text Window, which is situated at the top of the Text Panel, you can also add shapes, styles, and graphics.

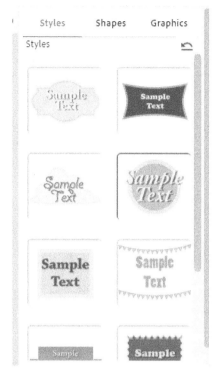

- To give your quote graphics style effects, use the **Styles Panel**.

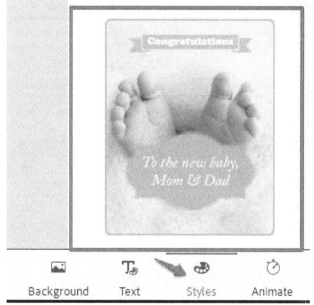

- Use **Animate** to give your text life. Any of the presets that are available to you can be chosen.

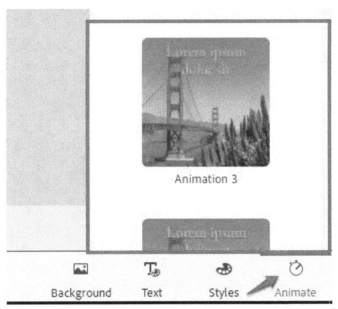

- Once your revisions are complete, click **Done** to apply your modifications, then click **Save** to save and export your project.

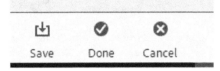

Creating Photo Books

Follow these steps to make a photo book.

- Once you click **Create**, a list of options will appear on your screen. Choose **Photo Book**.

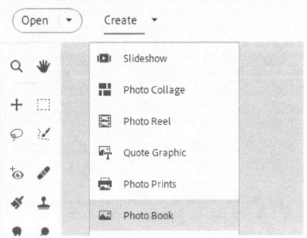

- Complete the following fields in the Photo Book dialog box, then click OK:

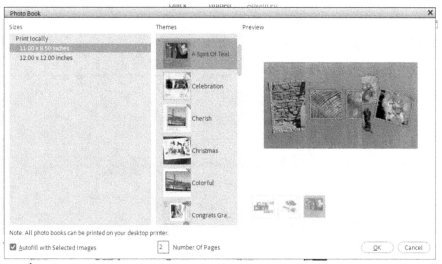

- ✦ Choose the size of the photo book under SIZES.
- ✦ Select a theme template under THEME.
- ✦ Choose **Autofill with selected images** to use the photos you have chosen in the Photo Bin.

> ☑ Autofill with Selected Images

- ✦ Specify the number of pages in the picture book (between 2 and 78).

> 2 | Number Of Pages

- The following choices are accessible in the project's lower-right corner:

> 📄   ▦   ＋
>
> Pages   Layouts   Graphics

- ✦ **Pages** present the pages of the picture book.

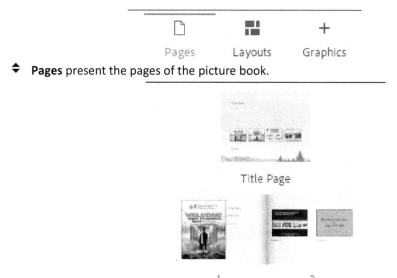

Title Page

- ✦ **Layout** shows the picture book's organizational structure.

Different Layouts

- ⬍ You can change the photo book's background, frames, and other visual components using **Graphics**. Include graphics if necessary.

  > Backgrounds

  > Frames

  > Graphics

- After finishing your changes, click **Done** to save and export your project, and then click **Save** to apply your changes.

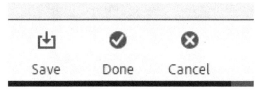

Creating Greeting Cards

To make greeting cards, complete the following.

- After choosing **Create**, select **Greeting Card**.

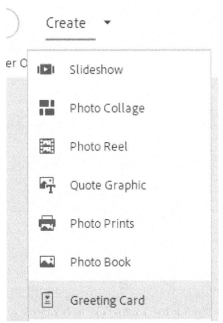

- After making the necessary adjustments in the **Greeting Card** dialog box, click OK

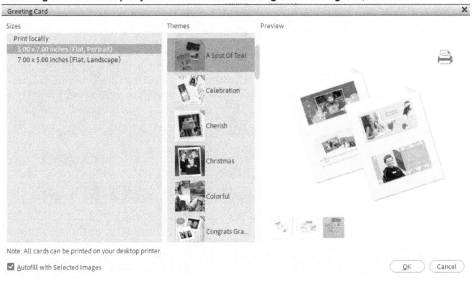

- To save your greeting card, click **Save**.

Creating Photo Calendars

To create a Photo Calendar, follow these steps.

- After choosing **Create**, select **Photo Calendar**.

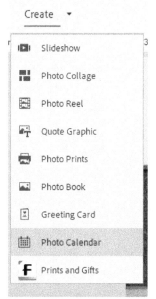

- Follow these steps in the Photo Calendar dialog box, then click **OK**

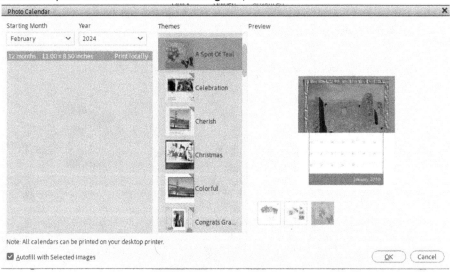

✦ Decide where you want your calendar's date (Year and Month) to begin.

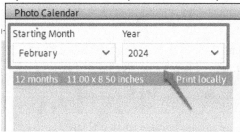

✦ Select the size of the photo calendar.

- Select a theme.

Themes

- Choose Autofill with selected images to use the photographs you have picked in the Photo Bin.

  Note: All calendars can be printed on your desktop printer.

- The options listed below are available in the lower-right corner of the project:

Pages	Layouts	Graphics

- **Pages**: shows the Photo Calendar's pages.
- **Layout**: Displays how the picture calendar is arranged.
- **Graphics**: This allows you to alter the picture calendar's backdrop, frames, and graphics.
- After you`re done with the necessary edits, click **Save** to import and save your project.

Save   Close

CHAPTER SEVEN

BASIC IMAGE RETOUCHING AND TRANSFORMATION IN PHOTOSHOP ELEMENTS I

Fixing Photographs

In many cases, your pictures may not come out the way you want when you take them with a camera or download them from a website. One of the major fixes to do to a photograph is *Resizing*, *Cropping*, *Straightening*, and many more. You will learn most of them in this chapter.

NOTE: To apply any fixing effect, be sure to have the desired image opened in your Photo Bin

Moving and Scaling Photographs
Do the following to move and scale a photograph.

- Open the Guided Mode in the Photo Editor. Click **Move & Scale Object** after selecting **Basics**.

- At the left side of the upper workspace, select the type of view you desire. It is advisable to choose any of the **Before & After** previews.

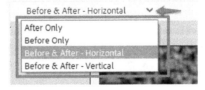

- Mark the object with a box by dragging it with the **Auto Selection Tool** (For things with clear edges, this is the best option) or You can make accurate selections with the help of the **Quick Selection Tool.**

- Use the **Brush Slider** to adjust the size of the brush for selection.

- **Add/Subtract** might help you narrow down your choices.

- Drag the chosen object to the desired location after selecting the **Move** or **Duplicate** button.

- To scale the object, drag its corners.

- When you move an object, built-in AI fills up the background behind it. With a few clicks of the **Healing Brush** or **Clone Stamp tool**, you may erase any blemishes.

- To save, click Next. Proceed with editing in Expert or Quick mode. Print or distribute this document.

Resizing A Photograph

Do the following to resize a photograph/image.

- After opening the image in the Photo Editor, select **Image** in the **File Menu**.

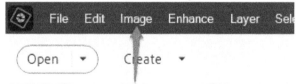

- From the drop-down list select **Resize** and click on **Image Size.**

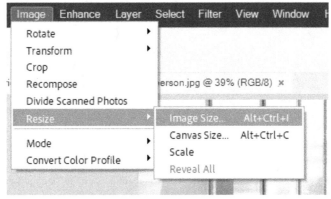

- Change the size of pixels using the **Width** and **Height** boxes in **Pixel Dimensions**. Click the drop-down arrow **beside** Pixels to change the unit of measurement.

- Change the size of the image using the Width and Height Boxes in Document Size. Click the drop-down arrow **beside** Pixels to change the unit of measurement.

- You can also try out other editing options available in the dialog box.

- After making the required modifications, click **OK**.

Extend Background

Do the following to extend the background of a photograph.

- After choosing your picture, open the **Guided Mode.**

- Choose **Special Edits**, and select **Extend Background**.

- In the **Choose Your Section**, click on **Set Canvas Size** to choose the preset size you want or create a custom size.

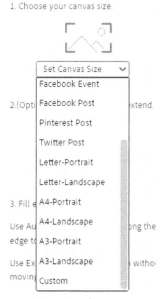

- Choose the photo's edges that you want to extend.

- Choose **Autofill** and allow artificial intelligence to work its magic in the background or **Extend** to manually make your edits.

3. Fill expanded area.

Use Autofill to clone content along the edge to fill the expanded area.

Use Extend to stretch the photo without moving the subject.

Autofill

Or

Extend

- If you happen to choose **Extend**, a brush appears for the edits you want to make.
  - Select **Protect** to keep the area you have brushed over undistorted while **Erase** allows you to cut out the selected portion.

Paint over the objects to prevent distortion.

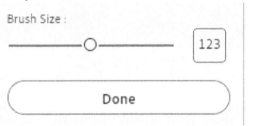

Protect   Erase

  - Use the **Brush Slider** to adjust the size of the brush, then select **Done**.

Brush Size :

———O——— 123

Done

- To remove any recurring patterns, fine-tune with a few clicks (not strokes) of the **Healing Brush** or **Clone Stamp tool**.

4. (Optional) Make minor fixes. For best results, keep the brush size as small as possible.

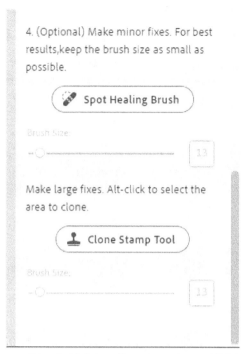

- Click **Next** to Save, continue editing in Quick or Expert mode, and Print or Share your file.

Removing Unwanted Objects

Do the following to remove unwanted objects in a photograph or image.

- Open the **Guided mode** of your photo. After choosing **Basics**, select **Object Removal**.

- To erase an object, paint over it with the **Brush tool**. Click **Remove Object** after that.

- Use the **Spot Healing Brush** and **Clone Stamp Tool** to adjust your outcome if needed. To delete an area, simply drag it over it. Use a small brush size to get the greatest effects.

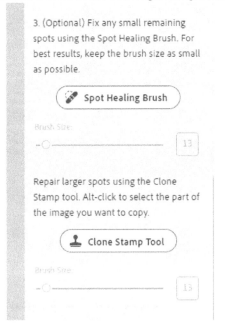

- o Use the **Spot Healing Brush** to correct little errors of omission and the **Clone Stamp Tool** to repair larger spots.
- Click **Next** to Save, continue editing in Quick or Expert mode, and Print or Share your file.

Replacing Backgrounds
Do the following to replace a background

- Open the **Guided Mode** of your **Photo Editor**.

- After choosing **Special Edits**, select **Replace Background**.

- To have your subject automatically selected, click the Select **Subject button** or manually select your subject by using the selection tools.

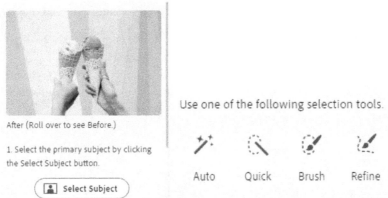

After (Roll over to see Before.)

1. Select the primary subject by clicking the Select Subject button.

Select Subject

Use one of the following selection tools.

Auto   Quick   Brush   Refine

- Do the following to select a different background.
  Click **Import A Photo** to add a photo to replace the background.

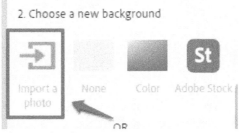

To create a transparent background, select **None**.

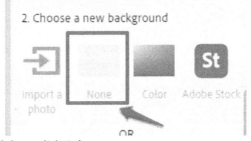

To add a color to the backdrop, click **Color**.

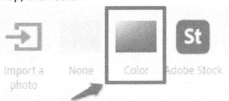

To apply a background setting, click **Preset**.

Choose Presets

- To move your subject or the background, use the **Move Tool**.

3. Use the Move Tool to reposition either
the subject or the background.

╋ Move Tool

- If necessary, paint over the foreground to sharpen the edges of your selection by selecting Refine Edge Brush.

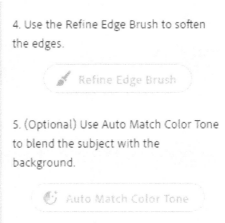

4. Use the Refine Edge Brush to soften
the edges.

Refine Edge Brush

5. (Optional) Use Auto Match Color Tone
to blend the subject with the
background.

Auto Match Color Tone

- Click **Next** to Save, continue editing in Quick or Expert mode, and Print or Share your file.

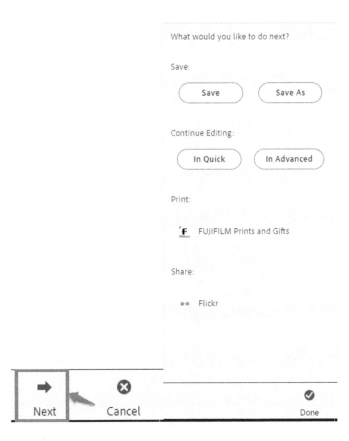

Cropping An Image

Cropping a photo can help eliminate distracting backgrounds and establish a clear focal point. Using the Crop tool is one of the simplest and fastest ways to crop an image.

To use the Crop tool, adhere to the guidelines provided below.

- From the Toolbar, choose the **Crop tool**.

- From the available **Tool Options**, choose the aspect ratio and resolution.

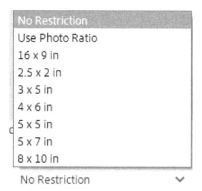

- ↕ **No Restriction**: This allows you to resize your image to any size.
- ↕ **Use Photo Ratio**: This helps to preserve the original aspect of the image while cropping.
- ↕ **Preset Sizes**: This gives you a variety of options for common photographic sizes.
- You can crop an image to the appropriate width and height by using the **Width (W)** and **Height (H)** parameters.

W: [　　　] ⇆ H: [　　　]

- **Crop Suggestion**: This provides you with four automated cropping recommendations for your picture or photo.

Crop Suggestions

- **Resolution**: This allows you to choose the desired resolution for your cropped image.

Resolution: [　　] Pixels/Inch

- The **Pixels/Ins** and **Pixels/Cm** options allow you to choose the preferred unit measurement.

Resolution: [　　] Pixels/Inch

- **Grid Overlay**: This helps to frame your photo before cropping. This choice consists of three parts: Grid, Rule of Thirds, and None.

Grid Overlay: ☐ ⊞ ▦

- Drag the crop marquee over the portion of the image you wish to keep, then release the mouse button when it shows as a bounding box with handles at the corners and size.

- To commit the operation, press the **Marker** button next.

Recomposing Images

Intelligent photo scaling is made easier with the Recompose tool, which preserves key visual elements like people, buildings, animals, and more.

Do the following to recompose images.

- To resize a photo, open it in the photo bin and choose the Guided option.

- Choose **Recompose** from the **Special Edits** menu in the **Guided Mode**.

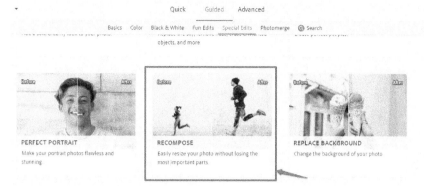

- Use the **Protect brush** to mark the areas that need to be protected. The locations designated for protection are shown in green. When you right-click on the image, you can choose from the following modes:

- o Use the Protect brush to mark the areas that need to be protected. When you right-click on the image, you can choose from the following modes:

  - o **Use Quick Highlight**: It is possible to rapidly identify the areas that need to be protected using this mode. Draw a circle around the subject to highlight the necessary areas. Trace the circle's perimeter, for instance, to emphasize the region inside the circle. The Quick Highlight feature makes sure that the circle's contents are designated as protected.
  - o **Use Normal Highlight**: Using this mode is similar to using a brush tool. Brush over any area that needs to be protected. To use Normal Highlight to protect a circle, for instance, the entire circle must be painted or marked.
- Select **Clear Protect Highlights** from the menu when you right-click the image to remove portions of the undesired marked areas.

- Use the **Remove brush tool** to mark the regions (unimportant areas) that you want to remove if you desire to remove any element in the photograph. The locations designated for protection are shown in red.

- Select **Clear Remove Highlights** from the menu when you right-click the image to remove portions of the undesired marked areas.

- To recompose your photo, drag the image handles or choose a size from the Preset drop-down menu.

- Click **Next** to Save, continue editing in Quick or Expert mode, and Print or Share your file.

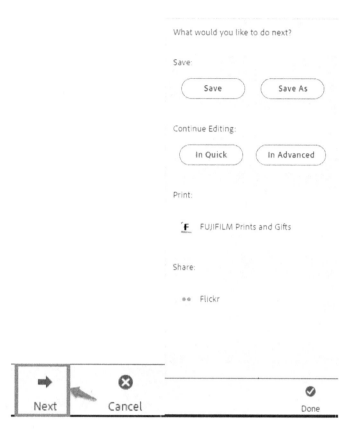

What would you like to do next?

Save:

Save   Save As

Continue Editing:

In Quick   In Advanced

Print:

F FUJIFILM Prints and Gifts

Share:

Flickr

Next   Cancel   Done

CHAPTER EIGHT

BASIC IMAGE RETOUCHING AND TRANSFORMATION IN PHOTOSHOP ELEMENTS II

Enhancing Photographs

Several methods are used to improve, edit, and fix images with Photoshop Elements. You can fix common problems including deleting extraneous objects and fixing scanned or broken images. You can also modify exposure levels to enhance photos that are fading or overexposed.

NOTE: To apply any fixing effect, be sure to have the desired image opened in your Photo Bin

Correcting Brightness And Contrast

- Open the **Guided mode** of your photo. After choosing **Basics**, select **Brightness and Contrast.**

- Select **Auto Fix** to make automatic correction.

- Adjust the **Brightness Slider** and the **Contrast Slider** to manually make your changes.

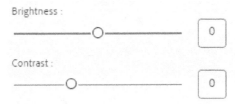

- Click **Next** to Save, continue editing in Quick or Expert mode, and Print or Share your file.

Correcting Skin Tone

- Open the **Guided mode** of your photo. After choosing **Basics**, select **Correct Skin Tone.**

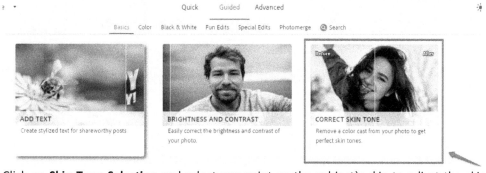

- Click on **Skin Tone Selection** and select any point on the subject's skin to adjust the skin tone based on that point.

- Adjust **Tan**, **Blush,** and **Light** to further edit the correction.

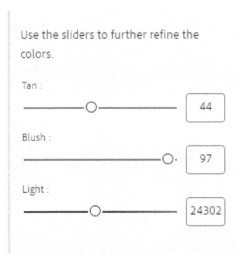

Use the sliders to further refine the colors.

Tan :

44

Blush :

97

Light :

24302

- Click **Next** to Save, continue editing in Quick or Expert mode, and Print or Share your file.

What would you like to do next?

Save:

Save   Save As

Continue Editing:

In Quick   In Advanced

Print:

F   FUJIFILM Prints and Gifts

Share:

••   Flickr

Next   Cancel   Done

Adjusting Photo Exposure

- Open the **Guided mode** of your photo. After choosing **Basics**, select **Lighten and Darken.**

- Click on **Auto Fix** to automatically correct the photo`s exposure.

- Use the **Shadow**, **Highlight**, and **Mid-tone** Slider to manually adjust the light exposure of the image.

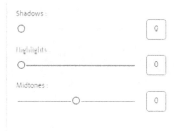

- Click **Next** to Save, continue editing in Quick or Expert mode, and Print or Share your file.

Enhancing Image Color
- Open the **Guided mode** of your photo. After choosing **Color**, select **Enhance Color.**

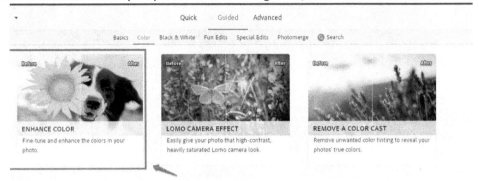

- Click on **Auto Fix** to automatically enhance the image.

- You can manually enhance the image`s color by adjusting the Hue, Saturation, and Lightness Slider.

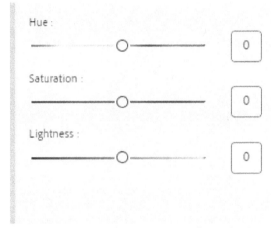

- Click **Next** to Save, continue editing in Quick or Expert mode, and Print or Share your file.

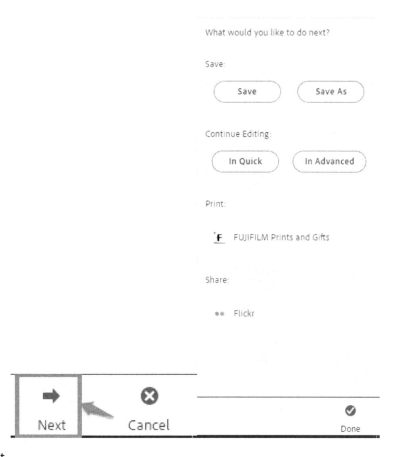

Removing Color Cast

Do the following to remove a color cast from a photograph.

- Open the **Guided mode** of your photo. After choosing **Color**, select **Remove A Color Cast.**

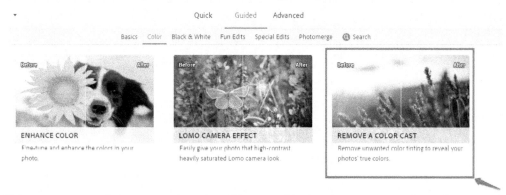

- Click on any area of the image that should be pure black, white, or grey after selecting **Color Cast Selection**.

Before

Remove a color cast from your photo by using the 'Color Cast Selection' tool below. Click on a part of the image that should be pure grey, white or Black.

- Click **Next** to Save, continue editing in Quick or Expert mode, and Print or Share your file.

Using Auto Fixes

With just one menu command, you can quickly adjust the lighting, contrast, and color of a photo with the Auto Fixes feature. Both the Quick and Advanced modes of the Enhance menu contain these commands.

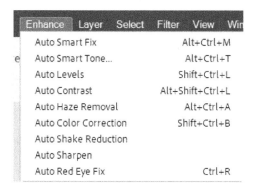

Auto Smart Fix

One effective technique for rapidly fixing common issues with saturation, contrast, and color balance is the Auto Smart Fix. **Alt+Ctrl+M** is the shortcut command for Auto Smart Fix.

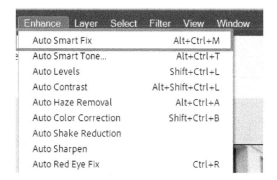

Auto Smart Tone

To alter the tonal values in your photo, use the Auto Smart Tone feature. **Alt+Ctrl+T** is the shortcut key combination.

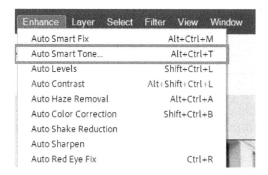

To make the most of this automated tool, follow these steps.

- When your image opens, select **Enhance** and then click **Auto Smart Tone**.

| Enhance | Layer | Select | Filter | View | Window |

Auto Smart Fix	Alt+Ctrl+M
Auto Smart Tone...	Alt+Ctrl+T
Auto Levels	Shift+Ctrl+L
Auto Contrast	Alt+Shift+Ctrl+L
Auto Haze Removal	Alt+Ctrl+A
Auto Color Correction	Shift+Ctrl+B
Auto Shake Reduction	
Auto Sharpen	
Auto Red Eye Fix	Ctrl+R

- For optimal adjustment, position the controller in the center of the image.

- The Auto Smart Tone can be changed by utilizing the **Three Dotted icons**.

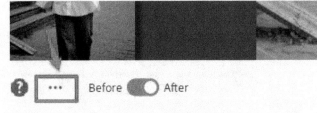

- To view previews, toggle the **Before/After** icon.

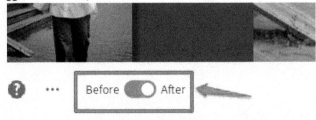

- To find out more about the tool, select the Learn from This Correction option, which is situated in the dialog box's lower-left corner.

- Choose **OK** to apply edits, **Reset** to all clear edits, and Cancel to end editing.

Auto Levels

With the Auto Level, one can alter an image's hue as well as its overall contrast. This program takes a picture and turns its lightest and darkest pixels to black and white, making the darkest portion of the image darker and the lightest portion lighter. **Shift+Ctrl+L** is its shortcut.

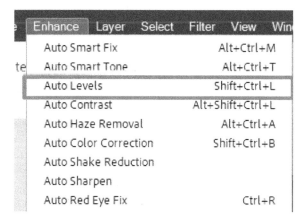

Auto Contrast

The Auto Contrast feature allows you to adjust an image's contrast without affecting its color. Photos that are hazy work well for this. Its shortcut is **Alt+Shift+Ctrl+L.**

Auto Haze Removal

You can clear the haze and fog out of your photos with Auto Haze Removal. If the haze removal tool in the Tools panel does not suit your needs, you may want to give it a try. **Alt+Ctrl+A** is the keyboard shortcut.

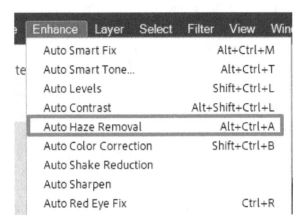

Auto Color Correction

By focusing on the shadows, highlights, and mid-tones of an image, Auto Color Correction can improve its color and contrast. This command can also be used to even out the color cast or adjust the color balance in your picture. The Keyboard shortcut is **Shift+Ctrl+B**.

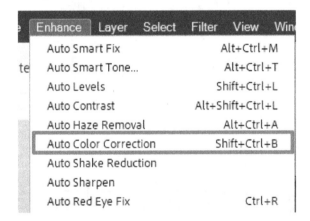

Auto Shake Reduction

The purpose of Auto Shake Reduction was to lessen the blur caused by camera movement. When required, this command comes in handy. Go to Enhance and select Shake Reduction for even more entertaining Shake Reduction options.

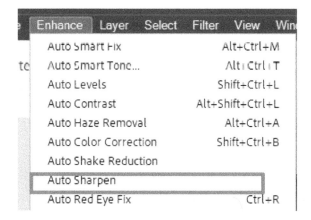

Auto Sharpen

Using the Auto Sharpen command, the focus of the image is sharpened by increasing pixel contrast. An excessively sharpened image appears noisy and grainy.

Auto Red-Eye Fix

To detect and eliminate red-eye from an image, utilize the Auto Red Fix command. A person or animal staring straight into the flash will get a crimson eye. The Red Eye tool is available in the Tools menu; use it if the Auto Red Eye feature isn't working. Command **Ctrl+R** is the shortcut.

CHAPTER NINE
BASIC IMAGE RETOUCHING AND TRANSFORMATION IN PHOTOSHOP ELEMENTS II

Retouching Photographs

Using a range of tools to edit and improve photographs is known as retouching in Photoshop Elements. Red-eye correction, tone adjustments, texture smoothing, spot, blemish, and undesired item removal are all possible.

For simple retouching, such as enhancing pictures and fixing typical flaws like closed eyelids, Adobe Photoshop Elements provides guided modes and unique edit features.

NOTE: To apply any fixing effect, be sure to have the desired image opened in your Photo Bin

Using Perfect Portrait
Available in the retouching command are features for *Removing Blemishes, Whitening Teeth, Smoothing skin, Opening Closed Eyes, Brightening Eyes,* and *Darkening Eyebrows.*

To access the Perfect Portrait Edit, open the **Guided Mode** in the **Photo Editor...**

and select **Perfect Portrait** under **Special Edits**.

Do the following to Smoothening Skins.

- After opening your photo in Perfect Portraits, select the type of view you desire at the left side of the upper workspace. It is advisable to choose any of the **Before & After** previews.

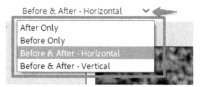

- Select **Smooth Skin** in the upper right of the workspace.

Before

1. Smooth Skin to reduce lines and blemishes.

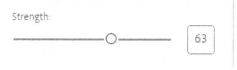

Note: For photos with multiple faces, click on one face and then the Smooth Skin button above. Repeat for each face.

- Use the **Strength Slider** to adjust the intensity of the smoothing effect.

Strength:

- To make the photo's contrast better, select **Increase Contrast**.

2. Increase contrast to add clarity.

Increase Contrast

Do the following to adjust the face of your subject in a photograph.

- Open your image in **Perfect Portrait** and select **Features**.

3. Adjust the facial features.

- In the **Adjust Face Features** dialog workspace, use the available options to tweak the face of your photograph.

- Use the **Lips** features to make adjustments to the lips of the subject.

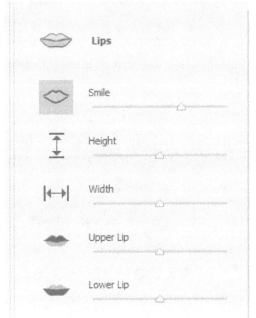

- **Eyes** allow you to adjust the subject`s eyes.

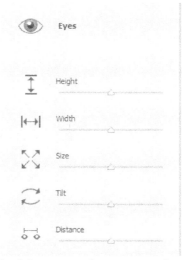

- Change the height and the width of the nose in the **Nose Panel**.

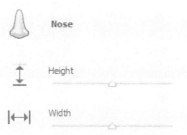

- Make adjustments to the shape of faces in the **Face Shape Panel**.

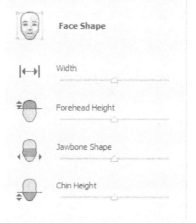

- Tilt the face of your subject using the options available in the **Face Tilt Panel**.

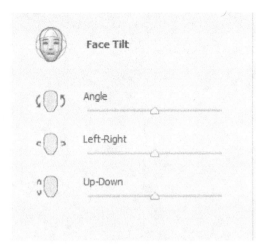

- Toggle the **Before/After** button to see the previews of the changes made to your subject.

- Click on **Reset** to return your image to its original state before the changes were made, **Cancel** to close the dialog box, and **OK** to apply your changes.

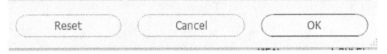

Do the following to **Remove Blemishes** to fix little flaws.

- After opening your photo in Perfect Portraits, select the type of view you desire at the left side of the upper workspace. It is advisable to choose any of the **Before & After** previews.

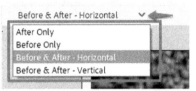

- Select **Remove Blemishes.**

- Reduce the size of your brush to a minimal one using the **[ ]** buttons and carefully paint over the image till you achieve your goal.

To whiten the teeth of your subject, do the following.

- After opening your photo in Perfect Portraits, select the type of view you desire at the left side of the upper workspace. It is advisable to choose any of the **Before & After** previews.

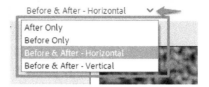

- Select **Whiten Teeth.**

- Paint over the teeth of your subject and the AI system does the rest.

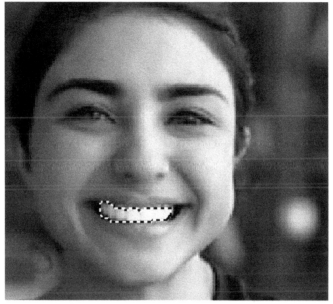

Do the following to open the closed eyes of a subject.

- After opening your photo in Perfect Portraits, select the type of view you desire at the left side of the upper workspace. It is advisable to choose any of the **Before & After** previews.

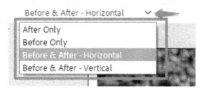

- Select **Open Closed Eyes**.

- From the dialog box, select your source from the samples available or choose from your **Computer, Organizer,** or **Photo Bin**.

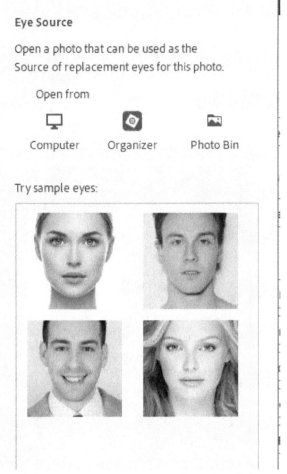

Eye Source

Open a photo that can be used as the
Source of replacement eyes for this photo.

Open from

Computer   Organizer   Photo Bin

Try sample eyes:

- Press and hold the **Before/After** button to receive sneak peeks of the modifications made to your photograph.

- Click on **Reset** to return your image to its original state before the changes were made, **Cancel** to close the dialog box, and **OK** to apply your changes.

To brighten eyes or darken the eyebrows, click on the commands and the actions will be carried out.

To add filter effects to your photograph in the Perfect Portrait, select **Add Glow** and select your glow filter from the dialog menu.

5. Add Glow to give the portrait a
Glamorous effect.

To shrink your subject without distortion, select Slim Down. Click as many times as necessary until you are happy with the outcome.

6. Click to Slim Down your subject
without distortion. Click again to Slim
further.

Restoring Old Photos
Do the following to restore old photos

- Open the **Guided Mode** in the **Photo Editor.**

Quick　　　Guided　　　Advanced

- Under the **Special Edit** category, select **Restore Old Photo.**

- To select the area of the picture that you want to restore, use the **Crop (C) tool** and the rotatable cropping frame.

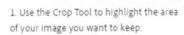

1. Use the Crop Tool to highlight the area of your image you want to keep.

- To fix tiny tears, lines, and spots, use the **Spot Healing tool.**

- To repair a damaged area of an image with an intact portion of the same shot, use the **Healing Brush tool**. To move a chunk of the image to the damaged area, press Alt + Click on a suitable area and drag it there.

Repairs bigger tears and scratches. Alt+Click to select the part of the image to be used for repairing.

- To duplicate a portion of an image to another, use the **Clone Stamp Tool**. Press Alt + click the source area, then drag on the damaged area to restore areas.

Copies one part of your image to
another. Alt+Click to select the part of
the image to be copied.

- To smooth out the portions of the picture with unwanted granulation, use the **Blur tool**.

Used for smoothing out imperfections.

- To fix tiny lines, dust impressions, and other flaws, use the **Dust Remover tool.**

3. Click on the Dust Remover button to
remove dust and scratches from your
image.

- To make adjustments to levels, contrast, and color, use the accessible buttons. With only one click, you can easily turn the picture into a black-and-white version.

4. Improve the color and contrast of your
image using following buttons :

- To improve the final product's clarity, use the **Sharpen tool**.

5. (Optional) Click on the Sharpen button
to increase the sharpness of your image.

- Click **Next** to select your preferred course of action once you've achieved the desired outcome.

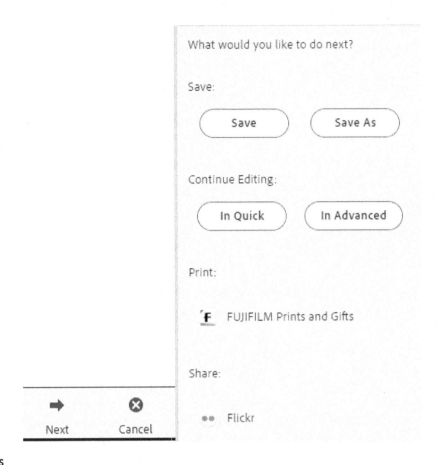

Replacing Skies

Perfect landscape is the command in the Guided mode to carry out this function. You may quickly and effectively replace skies, eliminate haze, and remove undesirable items with the Perfect Landscape guided edit.

Do the following to use Perfect Landscape.

- After choosing your picture, open the **Guided Mode.**

- Choose **Special Edits**, and select **Perfect Landscape.**

- If necessary, use the workspace's Crop and Straighten tools to make any necessary adjustments to your photo.

1. Click the Crop or Straighten Tool to adjust your photo.

- To remove the haze present in the photo, click on **Remove Haze**.

- Choose a new sky background from the presets available in the workspace.

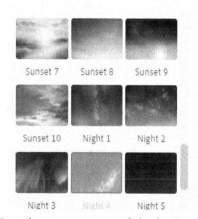

3. Choose a new Sky.

Sunset 7	Sunset 8	Sunset 9
Sunset 10	Night 1	Night 2
Night 3	Night 4	Night 5

- Use the **Opacity Slider** to adjust the transparency of the background and the **Brightness Slider** to manipulate the degree of light on the photo.

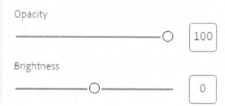

Opacity [100]

Brightness [0]

- Select **Auto Match Color Tone** to blend the color and tone of the subject and the new background.

☐ Auto Match Color Tone

- Use the **Move tool** to reposition the sky background.

＋ Move

- Use the **Shift Edge Slider** to adjust the accuracy and application of the sky background on the original image.

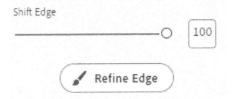

- Make quick adjustments with the **Spot Healing Brush Tool**; for best results, use the smallest brush size feasible.

Removing Scratches and Blemishes
Do the following to remove scratches and blemishes.

- Open the **Guided Mode** in the **Photo Editor.**

Quick   Guided   Advanced

- Under the **Special Edit** category, select **Scratches And Blemishes.**

- To remove minute stains and make minor corrections, use the **Spot Healing Brush Tool.**

- Use the **Healing Brush Tool** to fix larger image flaws.

2. Fix larger flaws in the Image using the Healing Brush. Alt + Click on a good area of the image & drag over the flaw to dissolve it.

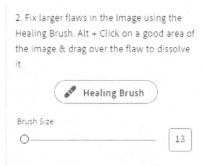

- After making the necessary edits, Select **Next**.

Blurring Out Backgrounds

By opacifying the surrounding environment, the Depth of Field effect lets you concentrate on specific regions of the picture and blurring out the other parts.

- Click **Depth of Field** in the **Special Edits** area while in **Guided mode**.

- Select **Simple** or choose Custom to manually define the object in focus and make your edits.

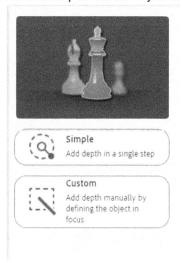

- If you chose Custom, use the selection tool to mark the portion you want the focus to be positioned in.

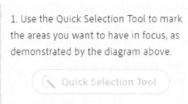

1. Use the Quick Selection Tool to mark the areas you want to have in focus, as demonstrated by the diagram above.

Quick Selection Tool

- Use **Add Blur** to blur out the other parts of the image and the **Blur Slider** to adjust the intensity.

2. Add Blur to the image, using the button below; to create depth.

Add Blur

Use the slider to vary the blur intensity.

Blur :

1

- If you chose Simple, click **Add Blur** to blur out the photograph. All around the picture, there is a consistent blur.

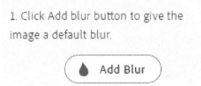

1. Click Add blur button to give the image a default blur.

Add Blur

- Click **Add Focus Area** and move the mouse over the desired focus areas on the image to specify the areas of focus.

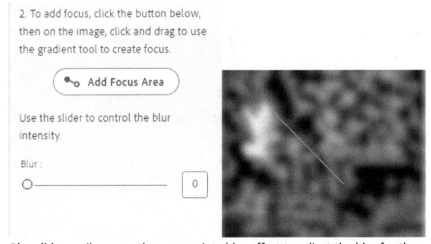

2. To add focus, click the button below, then on the image, click and drag to use the gradient tool to create focus.

Add Focus Area

Use the slider to control the blur intensity.

Blur :

0

- Drag the **Blur slider** until you get the appropriate blur effect to adjust the blur for the remaining portion of the image.

Use the slider to control the blur intensity.

Blur :

- Once you have the desired outcome, select your preferred course of action by clicking Next:

Next Cancel

Adding Dreamy Effects to Your Photograph
Your photos will appear dreamy thanks to the Orton effect.

Do the following to use the Orton Effect on your images.

- Click **Orton Effect** in the **Special Edits** area while in **Guided mode.**

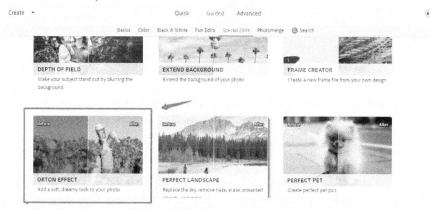

- Click **Add Orton Effect** to give your image a dreamy and gentle vibe.

Create a soft, dreamy feel for your photo using the Orton effect, originally created by Michael Orton. Click Add Orton Effect to apply the effect to the photograph.

- Modify the following settings to suit your needs:

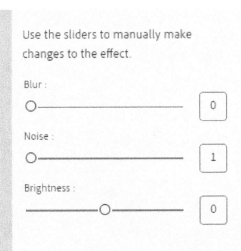

Use the sliders to manually make changes to the effect.

Blur :

0

Noise :

1

Brightness :

0

- o Define the degree of blur in the layer that is out of focus using the **Blur Slider**.
- o Use the **Noise Slider** to add noise to the blurred layer.
- o uses the **Brightness Slider** to increase the blurred layer's brightness.
- Once you have the desired outcome, select your preferred course of action by clicking Next:

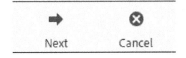

Next   Cancel

CHAPTER TEN

TURNING PHOTOGRAPHS TO LIVE VIDEOS

One of the amazing features to enjoy in Photoshop Elements is to animate still photographs or a part of an image. The Enhance menu contains three actions called *Moving Elements*, *Moving Overlay*, and *Moving Photos* that let you animate an image or a portion of a photograph in various ways.

Moving Elements

This moving feature allows you to animate a portion of an image.

Follow these steps to use Moving Elements.

- Once your picture is opened, choose **Moving Elements** from the **Enhance Menu**.

- Use the **Sky**, **Background**, or **Manual** selection tools in the dialog box to choose the area you want to add motion to.

Refine selection

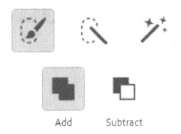

Add   Subtract

- Click the **Arrow Cursor** on the area you have selected for editing, then drag the mouse pointer in the desired direction.

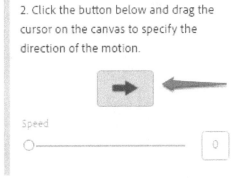

2. Click the button below and drag the cursor on the canvas to specify the direction of the motion.

Speed

0

- You can fine-tune the element's motion speed till you're satisfied by changing the speed slider.

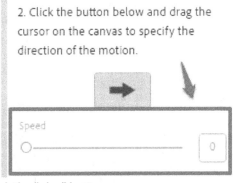

2. Click the button below and drag the cursor on the canvas to specify the direction of the motion.

Speed

0

- To see your sneak look, click the "play" button.

- Click **Export** to export your work once you are satisfied with the modifications you have made.

- You can export your file as a GIFF or an MP4 video file. To finally export your work, choose **Save**.

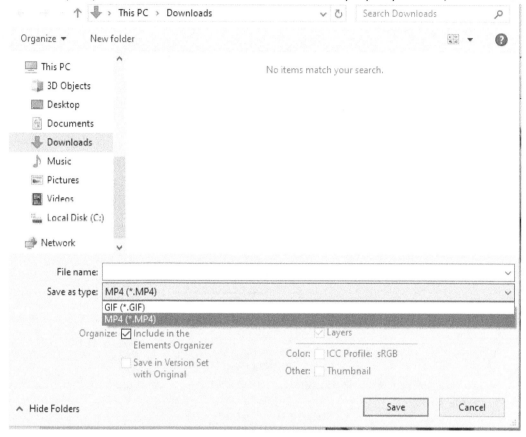

Moving Overlay

The Moving Overlay Command allows you to add overlay animations to your photo. Overlays, graphics, and frames are the three types of animated elements found in the Moving Overlay Command Center.

To add the moving overlays to your photo, follow these steps:

- Once the desired image has been opened, choose **Moving Overlays** from the **Enhance Menu**.

- On the right side of the dialog box, select **Overlays**, **Graphics**, and **Frames**—the three kinds of Overlay Animations you'll love to apply to your shot.

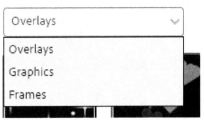

- You can prevent overlay adjustments from occurring to the subject of your shot by choosing **Protect Subject**.

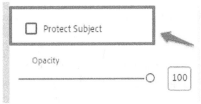

- Use the **Opacity Slider** to adjust the opacity of the additional animations.

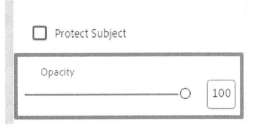

- Click the **Refine Overlay** option to adjust the position of your animation overlay.

- Click the Play button to see a sneak peek of your modifications.

- To export the image as an animated gif, click **Export** and adhere to the instructions. Choose **Save** after that.

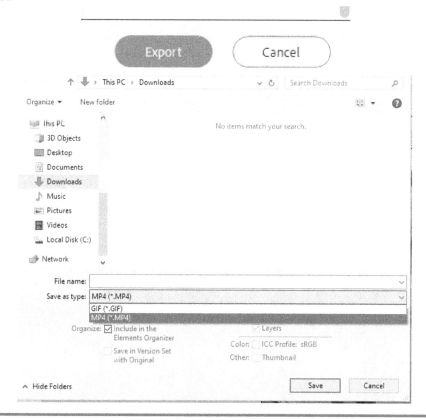

Moving Photos

With the Moving Photos command, you may take a picture and automatically apply a basic pan, zoom, or rotate effect. An animated gif can be exported from the image to make it move. Use the techniques listed below to create an animated image.

- Once the image you wish to animate has been opened, choose **Moving Photo** from the **Enhance Menu.**

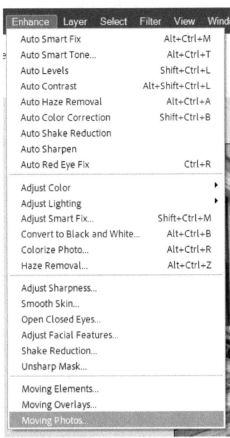

- To modify the **zoom** and pan of the preview image as needed, use the Zoom and Hand tools located on the right side of the dialog box.

- Double-click the Motion Effect options to apply them and see a preview of the effect appear on the image. The Motion Effects are located in the scrollable pane on the right side of the screen.

Double-click to apply effect

Zoom Out

Pan Left-Right

- Toggling the **3D Effect** on or off requires clicking the toggle button located at the bottom.

3D Effect

- To replay the effect preview once an effect has been played, click the Play button that shows up beneath the previous image.

- To export the image, click **Export** and then follow the instructions.

CHAPTER ELEVEN

THE CONCLUSION - A LETTER FROM TODD LEMMINGS

Congratulations to you!!!

That you have made it this far means you have come to the end of this book but not the end of the TIPS & TRICKS ON PHOTOSHOP ELEMENTS 2024. I hope you have been able to master the basic operations taught and discussed practically in this book.

Of course, you know that this manual guide is the first series of TIPS & TRICKS ON PHOTOSHOP 2024 by Todd Lemmings. To transform from being a novice and intermediate user of Photoshop Elements to being a master and a PRO then you should get the next series of this book. BOOK II: ADVANCED MASTERCLASS - TIPS & TRICKS ON PHOTOSHOP 2024 by TODD LEMMINGS which will be released on Tuesday, *20th Of February, 2024*.

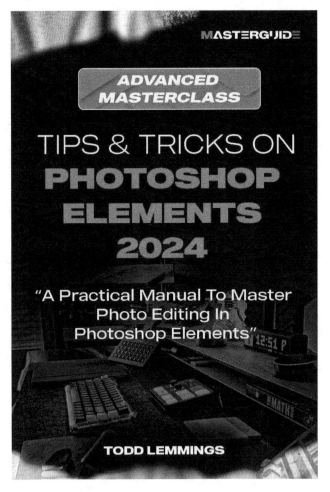

Made available in the next series are simplified advanced operations to master Photoshop Elements to become a PRO.

Below are some of the courses you will be exposed to.

- *File Handling in The Organizer.*
- *Saving Files in different file formats.*
- *Fixing Mistakes.*
- *Using Help in Photoshop Elements.*
- *The Dynamics of Layers in Photoshop Elements.*
- *Working with Selection Tools and Commands.*
- *Fixing Color, Contrast, and Clarity.*
- *Working with Filters and the Camera Raw Filter Plug-In*
- *How to use The Content-Aware Tool.*
- *Painting in Photoshop Elements*
- *How to use advanced Retouching Tools in Photoshop Elements.*
- *Working Texts and Shapes*
- *Troubleshooting and many more.*

INDEX